ALL THIS AND MOONLIGHT

BY

CHARLES R. JOHNSON

SAMUEL FRENCH, INC.

45 WEST 25th STREET   NEW YORK 10010

7623 SUNSET BOULEVARD   HOLLYWOOD 90046

LONDON   *TORONTO*

IMPORTANT BILLING AND CREDIT REQUIREMENTS

All producers of *ALL THIS AND MOONLIGHT* must give credit to the Author of the Play in all programs distributed in connection with performances of the Play and in all instances in which the title of the Play appears for purposes of advertising, publicizing or otherwise exploiting the Play and/or a production. The name of the Author *must* also appear on a separate line, on which no other name appears, immediately following the title, and *must* appear in size of type not less than fifty percent the size of the title type.

Please note:

Mention is made of songs which are *not* in the public domain. Producers of this play are hereby *CAUTIONED* that permission to produce this play does not include rights to use these songs in production. Producers should contact the copyright owners directly for rights.

ALL THIS AND MOONLIGHT was first
presented at the Triangle Theatre in New York
City. It was directed by the author, stage managed
by Anne M. Cantler, and it has the following cast:

ELLIE.................................Caris Corfman
NED...................................Jim Andreass
ANDREA............................ Melissa Weil
RICK..............................Marcus Giamatti
ALICE .... Gina Nelson
NORA................................Anne Chapin

CHARACTERS

Ned

Ellie

Andrea

Rick

Alice

Nora

SETTING

The action takes place in Ned's loft, and in various locations in and around New York City.

<h1 style="text-align:center">ACT I</h1>

AT RISE: NED is taking vegetables from a bag, polishing them with a cloth, and arranging them on a glass-top table. ELLIE is pacing behind the couch. SHE has a shawl around her shoulders.

ELLIE. (*Dramatically.*) "When I was a little girl, my father and mother used to travel with the fair. They gave performances, very good ones. And I would do the 'salto mortale' and all sorts of tricks. And when Papa and Mama died, a German lady took me to live with her and gave me lessons. When I grew up, I became a governess. But where I come from, and who I am, I don't know. Or who my parents were — perhaps they weren't even married ..."

NED. (*Looks up from his vegetables.*) Is a gourd a vegetable or a fruit?

ELLIE. "I don't know. I know nothing at all."

(NED exits.)

ELLIE. "I'd like so much to talk but there's not anyone. I haven't anyone." (*Screams and throws herself on the couch. SHE picks up a book.*)

(*NED reenters with his camera. HE climbs underneath the table and photographs the vegetables up through the glass.*)

ELLIE. What am I doing? I have absolutely no idea at all what I'm doing. Ok. My father and mother traveled the fairs. I did salto mortale, whatever that is ...

NED. Research. You've done impeccable research.

ELLIE. Shut up. (*Reading.*) "But where I come from and who I am, I don't know. Or who my parents were — perhaps they weren't even married. She takes a cucumber out of her pocket and begins to eat it." (*Reaches over and takes Ned's cucumber off the table.*)

NED. Hey!

ELLIE. "I don't know." (*SHE takes a bite.*) "I know nothing at all." Ooohh. I wonder if she peeled it first?

NED. Doesn't it say, "She whips out her potato peeler ..."

ELLIE. I'm supposed to be cleaning my rifle, not making a salad.

NED. You're cleaning a rifle, while eating a cucumber? What are you playing?

ELLIE. I'm a governess.

NED. Oh ... Right. (*A beat.*) Who wrote this brilliant play?

ELLIE. Chekhov.

NED. No need to get hostile.

ELLIE. Sorry. (*A beat.*) I know it has something to do with being alone and the plea for human contact.

(*NED takes Ellie's photograph.*)

ELLIE. Now please Ned, leave me alone. I don't need your help.

(*NED snaps a few photographs without looking through the lens.*)

ELLIE. I'm sorry, Ned. I'm just trying to prepare this audition, and I haven't the faintest idea why I'm eating a cucumber.

NED. (*A beat.*) Maybe you're hungry. (*Climbs back underneath the table.*)

ELLIE. I don't want to pry into your professional life, Ned, but what are you doing underneath the table?

NED. Photographing vegetables.

ELLIE. Oh ... Right.

NED. I'm trying to make my produce look different from everyone else's. I figure if I photograph them up through the glass, the vegetables will look like they're floating.

ELLIE. Floating vegetables?

NED. Clever, huh?

ELLIE. However did you come up with this original idea?

NED. Last New Year's Eve. I watched the New Year float in.

ELLIE. Research. You've done impeccable research. (*A beat.*) Ned ... (*SHE speaks to him through the glass of the table.*)

NED. (*Snaps her picture.*) Floating Ellie.

ELLIE. I'm sorry I wasted your afternoon.

NED. You needed to work on the monologue, didn't you?

ELLIE. Yeah.

NED. Besides, I've enjoyed hearing about your Russian upbringing. It was rather scandalous.

ELLIE. Do you think I'm wasting my afternoon preparing for this audition?

NED. I don't think that a governess sitting around chewing a cucumber, cleaning her weapon, is necessarily wasting her time. I myself had a very strict nanny who insisted that we eat our greens.

ELLIE. Did you?

NED. But not at gunpoint.

ELLIE. (*A beat.*) Get under the table.

NED. She did a pretty mean salto mortale ... whatever that is.

ELLIE. Go back under the table. (*A beat.*) Maybe it's New York. It's so competitive. I should have stayed back home. I'd probably be farther along by now. Perhaps I should have stayed in school. I don't know. I don't know anything at all.

(*A moment of silence, then NED bursts into applause.*)

ELLIE. What? What's that for? Neddie Edwards, here I am pouring my heart out to you and this is the response I get.
NED. (*A good imitation.*) "Oh, Neddie. Am I lousy actress, Ned? Perhaps I should give it all up. Move back to the farm. Perhaps I'm not any good. Perhaps I don't have what it takes. Perhaps my parents weren't even married." (*HE takes a bite out of the cucumber and shoots his imaginary gun.*)

(*ELLIE bursts out in laughter and jumps up on the couch and hits him with pillows.*)

NED. Break time! (*Jumps up and leaves the room.*)
ELLIE. I hate it when you see through me.
NED. (*Offstage.*) I've been seeing through you since you were fourteen and chubby.
ELLIE. I was never chubby. (*We hear a jazzy Gershwin tune.*) I was a little on the plump side ...

(*NED reenters. HE is wearing sunglasses and a black fedora. HE struts around the room ... playing the bass, the saxophone; the back of the couch becomes a piano.*)

NED. I have photographs.

ELLIE. Burn them.
NED. No way.
ELLIE. At least I didn't dress like a geek in high school.
NED. A geek?
ELLIE. You used to wear black turtleneck sweaters every day of the week.
NED. I was going through a phase. Besides, Rosamund Threlkeld said they made me look like a young Hemingway.
ELLIE. And you believed her?
NED. You believed you were only plump.
ELLIE. (*A pause.*) What if they ask me at the audition why I'm cleaning my rifle? What am I supposed to say?
NED. (*A beat.*) It was dirty.

(*NED puts the hat on Ellie's head.*)

ELLIE. I want this part, Ned.
NED. You want everything.
ELLIE. I do. (*SHE dances around the room.*)

(*NED sits and watches her. HE munches on the cucumber.*)

ELLIE. I want a big apartment on Central Park West. I want to eat ice cream all day long. I want to be a big Broadway actress.
NED. You eat ice cream all day long, you will be.

ELLIE. I want to do Shakespeare in the park every summer. I want to do films. I want to go to Cannes.

NED. Where?

ELLIE. Cannes.

NED. You just like saying it.

ELLIE. Cannes.

NED. Constantly mobbed by your adoring fans. Your hand forever cramped from signing autographs.

ELLIE. I read in this magazine that a certain major film star refuses to sign autographs ever since someone approached him in the men's room while he was standing at the urinal ...

NED. That's lousy. I mean if you can scribble a limerick, you can sign your name.

ELLIE. It's true.

NED. Who? Tell me, who?

ELLIE. Well, I hate to gossip ... (*SHE whispers to him.*)

NED. No ... You're kidding?

ELLIE. (*A beat.*) Neddie? (*SHE sits beside him.*)

NED. Yo ...

ELLIE. Thanks for cheering me up.

NED. Any time.

ELLIE. I know we kid a lot. But I really want it.

NED. His autograph? Just peel it off the salad dressing bottle.

ELLIE. You know what I mean.

NED. I do. (*A beat.*) I think you'll get it.

ELLIE. But I want to be good at it, too. I want to be a good actress.

NED. You are. Just be sure to keep your rifle clean and eat your greens. (*HE hands her the cucumber.*)

ELLIE. And I want you right there with me ... pulling me back down to earth.

NED. You don't want much, do you?

ELLIE. (*Kisses him.*) Ned ... Do you ever feel like someday, someone will walk through the door and blow the whistle on us?

NED. Why? What are we doing?

ELLIE. You know what I mean. We're not there yet, but someday we will be. And when that day comes, do you think everyone will know that underneath we're just plain old you and me?

NED. I won't tell as long as you don't.

ELLIE. It'll be our little secret.

(*THEY kiss. The door BUZZER sounds. NED jumps.*)

NED. Oh, God! It's my date!

ELLIE. Who?

NED. My date. I have a date tonight! (*Runs around the room straightening up. HE puts the vegetables in the bag.*) Look, Ellie, you've got to get out of here.

(*SHE stares at him but doesn't make a move.*)

NED. Please, go. Please.

(*The BUZZER sounds.*)

NED. I can't keep her waiting in the hall. What will she think?

(*ELLIE starts off.*)

NED. Wait ... take this stuff with you. (*Calling out.*) Be right there! (*Hands her the playscript and his bag of vegetables.*)
ELLIE. See you at the "ten year." (*SHE turns to exit, but stops. SHE runs back into his arms and kisses him again.*)
NED. No, no, no ... (*HE's not doing a good job of fighting her off.*) You have to go now. You can't stay here. Do you hear me? I have a girl waiting in the hall!

(*ELLIE stops kissing him. SHE very simply turns and exits. NED turns in the other direction and ANDREA enters.*)

ANDREA. Hello.
NED. Hello.
ANDREA. Am I your first?
NED. Sorry?
ANDREA. Blind date?
NED. Oh ... yes.

ANDREA. I could tell. I'm getting to be a pro at it.

NED. Andrea, isn't it?

ANDREA. (*Correcting his pronunciation.*) An*drea*. My friends call me Andy, but I hate that.

NED. How sad. Well, come in. Sit down. Sorry to keep you waiting so long.

ANDREA. It's ok. You called out. Sometimes when I buzz I have the feeling that the guy checks me out through the peephole and then decides to be called out of town on business. I hate that, too.

NED. I can see why you would. Andrea, may I get you a drink?

ANDREA. An alcoholic drink?

NED. Sure.

ANDREA. No, thanks. I don't drink yeast. Most alcohol has yeast in it. Did you know that?

NED. I didn't know that.

ANDREA. Well, it does. No, thanks.

NED. How about soda? I'm sure soda is yeast free.

ANDREA. Sugar. Caffeine. Syrups. Artificial sweeteners. Preservatives. I'll pass.

NED. You're pretty much a health conscious kinda person.

ANDREA. (*A beat.*) I'm hypersensitive!

NED. I wouldn't say that. More people should be aware of the chemicals they put in their body. How about some water?

ANDREA. Bottled?

NED. No, tap.

ANDREA. I guess that will be ok. Do you mind if I look around? You can tell a lot about a guy from the way he keeps house.

NED. No. Not at all.

ANDREA. (*As she exits.*) I went out with a guy last week who had a pet monkey chained to his bedpost. The world is full of sick people.

NED. I'll get the water. (*HE exits. Calling from offstage.*) Do you want anything in it? Andrea?

ANDREA. (*Offstage.*) No. What would you put in water?

(*ELLIE enters and lies down on couch.*)

NED. (*Offstage.*) Ice.

ANDREA. No. Bad for the digestion. Nice closet space.

NED. (*Entering.*) I cut up some fresh vegetables earlier ... Ellie!

ELLIE. I would like a big yeasty martini, please. And some peanuts for my monkey. (*SHE takes a bite off her cucumber.*)

NED. What are you doing here? I thought I told you to leave.

ELLIE. I did. Then I came back. I wanted to meet Aan-dree-ya.

NED. (*Correcting her.*) An*drea*.

ANDREA. (*Offstage.*) Yes?

NED. How about that view! Ellie, you're in the way.

ELLIE. Nice way to talk to the woman you love.

(*NED turns his back on Ellie. SHE stands and exits. ANDREA enters.*)

ANDREA. What was this building used for before they let people live here?

NED. A cigar factory, I think.

ANDREA. I knew it. You can still sort of smell it in the air.

NED. Really? I have never noticed.

ANDREA. That's because you live here. You've grown used to it. It's amazing what people will tolerate.

NED. Here's your water.

ANDREA. Thank you, Ned.

NED. See any monkey business?

ANDREA. You keep your shoes in pairs, but not in a row.

NED. I'm sorry.

ANDREA. No, that's good. It means that there's order to your life but you're not excessively anal. Here's a quarter I found under your bed.

NED. Thank you.

ANDREA. You said on the phone you're a photographer? Is this a hobby? Or can you make a living at it?

NED. I manage to do all right.

(*THEY sit silently awkward for a moment.*)

NED. Would you like to see some of my work?

ANDREA. Sure.

NED. Well, let me think what I have to show you. (*HE grabs a tray of slides and arranges them on the light box.*) This is some stuff I'm still editing. You can get a better view if you look through the loupe.

ANDREA. The what?

NED. This eyepiece. It's called a loupe.

ANDREA. I've seen jewelers with these.

NED. Something like them, yes.

ANDREA. (*SHE looks a minute then.*) Have you thought about going into video?

NED. No.

ANDREA. You really should. It is the future.

NED. So, Andrea ... you hungry? I'm starved.

ANDREA. No, not really.

NED. Not even just a little?

ANDREA. No.

NED. Did you want to do something first and then have dinner?

ANDREA. We could. Although I don't really care if we eat at all.

NED. Had a late lunch?

ANDREA. No.

NED. Then what is it? Are you not feeling well? I mean, if you're not feeling well, we can do this some other time.

ANDREA. I'm fine. In fact, this is the best I've ever felt.

NED. You don't eat ... You don't drink ... Why not?

ANDREA. Allergies.

NED. Allergies?

ANDREA. I'm hypersensitive! I'm taking this battery of tests to find out which food groups my body cannot tolerate.

NED. Do you get a rash or something?

ANDREA. Are you kidding me? My body goes into violent spasms. I get all swollen. I turn bright red, and my blood pressure jumps sky high.

NED. Damn ... That's scary. What can you do about it?

ANDREA. I don't eat the foods that cause it. No dairy products, no poultry, no grains, nothing grown in the ground or directly on top of it. Like potatoes, carrots, strawberries, watermelon ... Something to do with dirt, I don't quite get it. And above all, no animals.

NED. For pets, or for lunch?

ANDREA. Either.

NED. What can you eat?

ANDREA. Oh, lots of things. I can have fish.

NED. Well, that's good. Fish is supposed to be very good for you, too.

ANDREA. I hate it. I gag if I just smell fish.

NED. (*A beat.*) For instance, what did you have for breakfast today?

ANDREA. I didn't have breakfast. I never have breakfast.

NED. Ok. Ok ... Neither did I. Lunch ... I had a hot dog with everything on it. I suppose you can't eat a hot dog?

ANDREA. Are you kidding? Call the morgue! First of all, it's meat. And even that's debatable. I can't eat bread—which eliminates the bun.

NED. Mustard, ketchup ...

ANDREA. Chemicals.

NED. Onions.

ANDREA. Dirt.

NED. Pickles?

ANDREA. Oh, I can have pickles.

NED. Well, that's good. That's something.

ANDREA. Depending on how they're prepared. For lunch today, I had an apple and some raisins. But if you want to get something ...

NED. No ... no. Personally, I don't see why you haven't starved by now.

ANDREA. I eat as much as I want, really. Besides, I'm too busy working to eat.

NED. What do you do?

ANDREA. I'm an aerobic instructor. Low impact. So what would you like to do this evening?

NED. Well, let me think a minute.

(*A pause. ELLIE enters.*)

ELLIE. Let's force a Hershey bar down her throat and watch the silly bitch burst!

NED. I thought I told you to go away.

ELLIE. I tried. But I just couldn't miss this.

(*ANDREA takes no notice of Ellie or of Ned's talking to her.*)

ELLIE. I just don't think she's the right girl for you, Ned.

NED. You think that, do you?

ANDREA. We could go to a movie.

NED. Now there's an idea.

ELLIE. I just can't see you falling for a girl like this.

NED. Like what?

ANDREA. Oh, I don't care, any movie.

NED. And who says I'm falling for her?

ELLIE. Why is she here?

NED. It's a date. A measly little blind date. (*To Andrea.*) I could do a movie.

ANDREA. You pick. I'm not too fussy about films.

ELLIE. As long as she doesn't have to eat them. Imagine Thanksgiving. Little Neddie junior saying grace. Mom under the table scouting loose change. Dad ceremoniously carving the Thanksgiving "pickle."

ANDREA. I'm not crazy about the films you have to read.

ELLIE. We call them *books,* Andrea.

ANDREA. Foreign films give me a headache.

NED. That's fine.

ANDREA. And I can do without the violence and the sex. Musicals are so unbelievable. Slasher films are out. Why do people make those? They make me sick. This guy I went out with last week took me to this suspense thriller, and I got so sick to my stomach ...

ELLIE. What has she got to lose? A couple of raisins.

(*NED slowly walks over to Ellie and kisses her.*)

ANDREA. I didn't know if it was the movie or the fact that he worked for the Bronx Zoo. He was the guy with the monkey. He had a glass eye – the monkey! Some people are so sick. (*SHE sneezes a few times. Then horrified ...*) Oh, my God! Are you wearing cologne?

(*NED and ELLIE break from their embrace.*)

NED and ELLIE. Call the morgue!

(*THEY kiss again as the LIGHTS BLACKOUT. They come up on RICK at a baseball game. Binoculars are glued to his eyes throughout most of the scene. After a moment, NED enters with food. HE is wearing a Yankee cap and jacket.*)

NED. Hey, what'd I miss?

RICK. Oh nothing. Nada. Not a damn thing. This must be the worst they've played ball all season long. (*NED hands RICK a hot dog.*) We're eating again?

NED. For some reason Rick, I can't seem to appease this craving for hot dogs.

RICK. It's the ball park. Sometimes I think the only reason I go to the ball game is to eat peanuts and drink beer. (*Looks through the binoculars.*)

NED. I'm sure that's the only reason. How come hot dogs always taste better at the ball park?

RICK. You've already said that today about the beer, the peanuts, the hot pretzels and the ice cream thing you ate.

NED. It's all part of enjoying the game. Besides, I'm eating to forget.

RICK. Forget what?

NED. That sister of your friend.

RICK. You finally called her? Well ... How'd it go?

NED. It didn't. She started having this sneezing fit and had to go to the hospital.

RICK. Ask her out again.

NED. I don't think so.

RICK. Why not? Was she pretty?

NED. Very pretty until she started sneezing.

RICK. Then what's the problem?

NED. Dirt!

RICK. What?

NED. She can't eat. She has these allergies. She never eats.

RICK. Ned ... do you realize how many guys would like to go out with a girl who doesn't eat? You don't know what you've got there.

NED. Huh?

RICK. Food is the major problem with dating. "Where will we go for dinner? How much can I get away with spending? What will I talk about? How much do I tip? How much can I eat and still be good for something later?" Ned, this girl is a find. Food is the biggest hassle in a relationship.

NED. "Relationship?" You never spend more than two weeks with any girl. You've had "relationships" where you've never gotten your boots off.

RICK. I have a short attention span.

NED. When you meet someone for the first time, until you find out if you have anything in common, you can eat and drink. Not Andrea.

RICK. Andrea? She sounds exotic. I don't think you gave this girl a chance.

NED. She doesn't drink alcohol.

RICK. (*A beat.*) We'll find you another girl. They're all over. Especially girls who like to eat and drink.

(*THEY both watch a fan walk by a few rows in front of them.*)

NED. Hey, great day for a ball game, huh?

RICK. The Yankees haven't seemed to notice. (*Looks back through the binoculars.*)

(*After a moment, THEY both jump up out of their seats. The crowd SHOUTS. Safe? No, out. THEY sit back down.*)

RICK. Here, here, here, check out these two girls behind third.

(*NED looks.*)

RICK. Huh? I get the blonde.

NED. Thanks. How come you always take the really good looking ones?

RICK. Hey, you know the rules. Whoever finds them, gets first choice. Besides, her friend was eating a snow cone, and I thought you found that attractive in women.

NED. You're just jealous because I'm more discriminating than you.

RICK. I have no idea what that means.

NED. It means that you'll probably get lucky tonight, and I won't.

RICK. You're right.

NED. And how did you trap your latest victim?

RICK. She was sitting next to you the whole first half of the ball game.

NED. She didn't stay very long.

RICK. She probably went home to get ready.

NED. (*Stands and stretches.*) Stand up. It's time to stand up.

RICK. I just stood up a little while ago.

NED. Who cares? This is the time to stretch, whether you have to or not.

RICK. (*Stands reluctantly.*) I forgot I was with the Pollyanna of baseball. You'll probably catch another ball today.

NED. Probably. (*A beat.*) So how did you charm this one?

RICK. The way I charm them all. I simple tell them that I work in the motion picture industry. It works every time.

NED. They're impressed that you make slasher movies?

RICK. Are you kidding? They like to scream. Get frightened. Be held real close. It's a turn-on.

NED. I suppose you tell them that you're a famous film director? And do they want a screen test?

RICK. Ned ... Ned, my boy. I don't have to lie to these girls.

NED. You don't?

RICK. No. I tell them the truth. When they ask what I do, I tell them that I'm a gaffer.

NED. And they're immediately impressed?

RICK. Always. No one has the slightest idea what a gaffer does. It just sounds so technical. I just have to be important.

NED. No one ever asks "What exactly does a gaffer do?"

RICK. No. Never. The next question is "What movie stars have you met?" I start the list and before you know it, it's the next morning. May we sit down now?

(*THEY sit.*)

NED. Do you compare them? Which one is better?

RICK. No, I don't have time. I'm too busy taking inventory. (*He looks through the binoculars.*)

(*THEY both jump up as the crowd SCREAMS.*)

RICK. Wow!

NED. Did he look safe to you?

RICK. I don't know, but check out his halter top at three o'clock. (*Hands Ned the binoculars.*)

NED. Oh, my God! She is running down the stairs.

RICK. Give 'em back. Give 'em back.

NED. Too late. (*Hands them back to Rick.*)

RICK. I don't see why you don't meet more women being a photographer. It's the same thing as being a gaffer. Use it. Women find it mysterious, glamorous. You must see gangs of models everyday.

NED. I don't like working with models.

RICK. Why not?

NED. They slow me down.

RICK. That's what I mean.

NED. No. It's much harder to get the shot you want. Whenever you work with a model you lose control. There's enough variables already, the weather, the light ...

RICK. You're going to be tough. But don't worry. I'll find someone. Let me give you Alice's number.

NED. Alice?

RICK. Nice girl. Wait till you see her.

NED. I don't know, Rick. I don't think I'm up for any more blind dates. Not just now.

RICK. She's not blind. You've already met her.

NED. Where? When?

RICK. My poker party last month. You asked me who she was?

NED. That's Alice. She was nice. Good looking. She had some big gorilla on her arm.

RICK. *Had* some big gorilla on her arm. It's now or never, Neddie.

NED. All right. All right. Give me her number.

RICK. You have to promise to call her.

NED. I'll call her. I'll call her.

RICK. Promise.

NED. I promise. (*A beat.*) Wave!

RICK. At who?

NED. No. It's a wave.

(*NED jumps up and starts to wave his arms. RICK reluctantly joins in. The LIGHTS fade and come up on NED seated in a restaurant. HE picks up a menu, glances at it. HE's read it before. HE pours himself a glass of wine. ELLIE enters.*)

ELLIE. Hi! Sorry I'm late. Got caught up in rehearsals. Never, I repeat never, do a play when the author is still living. Rehearsals are just that — a time to rehearse. Experiment. But when the author is present, you lose anything you've built to that point. They sit there, majestically. Don't say a word. Blank stare. Arms folded. And you know they're thinking this stupid actress is all wrong for my play. She can't act.
NED. Go away!
ELLIE. (*A beat.*) Then they look down at you over their glasses. Have you noticed all writers wear glasses? It's all effect. They don't like them. They either look over them or put them up on their head and squint. I hate it when people sit in judgement of you. I just hate it. So, how was your day?
NED. Go away!
ELLIE. Did you order for me? I'm not very hungry. I'll just pick a little off whatever you're having. What are you having?
NED. Leave me alone. I don't want you here.
ELLIE. And yet I'm here.
NED. (*Calling out.*) Could I get another table, please?
ELLIE. Now stop it. Settle down.

NED. You have to go away. I'm meeting someone for dinner.

ELLIE. A girl?

NED. Yes, a girl.

ELLIE. (*A beat.*) You mean to tell me, that you're having dinner with another girl here, at *our* restaurant?

NED. It's not *our* restaurant anymore. It's *my* restaurant now. So go away.

ELLIE. I'm glad you got this table. *Our* table. I have big news to tell you. May I have some wine, please?

(*NED pours her a glass.*)

ELLIE. Thank you. I don't know how to tell you this exactly. I have a feeling as soon as I tell you ...

(*NED closes his eyes and puts his fingers in his ears and recites baseball commentary. ELLIE stands and exits. After a moment, ALICE enters. SHE sees Ned and waits for him to see her.*)

ALICE. Ned? Ned Edwards?

NED. Huh? (*Looking up.*) Alice? Hi.

ALICE. Bonjour.

(*NED jumps up and pulls out Alice's chair for her.*)

ALICE. What a charming little bistro. Merci. (*SHE sits.*) You come here often?

(*ELLIE reenters, smiling.*)

NED. It's a favorite spot.

(*ELLIE waits for Ned to pull out a chair for her. HE sits in it. Undaunted, SHE pulls up a chair from another table.*)

ELLIE. Merci.

(*Again, only NED sees or hears Ellie.*)

ALICE. What were you doing when I came in? Are you all right?
NED. I'm fine. I'm fine. I was ah ...
ELLIE. This should be good.
NED. (*For Ellie's benefit.*) Hiccups. Old hiccup remedy.
ALICE. Really? Does it work?
NED. (*Looking at Ellie.*) Apparently not. I'm glad you were free tonight.
ALICE. Me, too.
NED. I ah ... took the liberty of ordering a bottle of wine. Are you a wine drinker?
ALICE. *Certainement.*
NED. I hope that means "yes." I ah ... already poured you a glass.

ELLIE. That was really my glass.

(*ALICE picks it up and sniffs the wine.*)

ELLIE. It's ok, you can have it.
NED. I wanted it to breathe.
ALICE. It's Bordeaux. It shouldn't really have to breathe. Only full-bodied wines really need to breathe. Like a Châtenuneuf-du-Pape or a Côtes du Rhône or a Petite Sirah.
NED. Really?
ELLIE. She's out of your league. You can't afford her.
ALICE. And there are those who debate even that. Some feel that any oxidation only expedites the process of decay.
NED. Perhaps I shouldn't have poured the wine.
ELLIE. (*Overlapping with Ned.*) I don't think you should have poured the wine. "Decay."
ALICE. I think there's always room for debate, don't you? Just tell people that you were "decanting" it for me. That's very chic to do these days.
NED. I'll remember that.
ELLIE. Très chic ...
NED. You can tell it's a Bordeaux just by smelling it?
ALICE. And from the shape of the bottle.
NED. Well, you're obviously a wine connoisseur. Now I'm glad I didn't order a beer.

ELLIE. "I knew it was a Bud from the shape of the bottle."

(*NED slams his fist down on the table. ALICE turns away, embarrassed.*)

NED. (*To Ellie.*) Would you please get out of here?

ELLIE. Why did you meet her here? You know this was our restaurant? You knew I'd come here too. (*A thought.*) Hey, maybe I'll show up. Maybe I'm here already.

(*NED stands and nervously looks around the room.*)

ALICE. You see someone you know?

NED. No. I don't. (*That's a relief. Back to Alice.*) Well, I hope you like this wine. It's one of their best.

ELLIE. And one of our personal favorites.

ALICE. I'm sure I will. Even if it is served in a burgundy glass.

ELLIE. I hope she chokes on it.

NED. I hope you're hungry? (*HE waits for a response.*)

ALICE. *J'ai faim.* (*Translating for him.*) I'm starved.

NED. That's just what I wanted to hear. (*Raising his glass.*) Chin. Chin.

ALICE. *Santé!*

(*THEY both drink.*)

NED. Well?
ALICE. (*Demonstrates her wine tasting technique.*) *C'est magnifique!*
ELLIE. She's a gem. Don't let this one get away.
ALICE. It's not bad for a cru.
NED. A what?
ALICE. A "Cru Bourgeois" Bordeaux. (*Looking at label.*) Oh look! *"Mis en bouteille à la propriété."*
NED. Really? What does that mean?
ELLIE. Bourgeois, bourgeois, bourgeois ...
ALICE. It means the same as "au château."
NED. (*A beat.*) And what does that mean?
ELLIE. Bourgeois, bourgeois ...
ALICE. It means that the wine maker bottles his own wine.
NED. Is that good?
ELLIE. Bourgeois ...
ALICE. Well, it means that we know we're drinking what the label says we're drinking. So often in Europe, if there is not a good *"negociant,"* cheap wine manufacturers can put classy labels on the bottles, then raise the price. Therefore, *"mis en bouteille a la propriété."* *N'est-ce pas?*
ELLIE. (*A beat.*) Where do you find these girls?

ALICE. I'm going to France next month. It's a wine tasters' travel package. We tour three of the four main vineyard areas: Champagne, Burgundy, and the Bordeaux region.

NED. Why not all four?

ALICE. The Mediterranean Languedoc is vastly inferior as far as wine goes.

ELLIE. (*Hitting Ned.*) Silly.

NED. Too bad.

ALICE. *Tant pis.*

NED. Luckily, you already know French.

ALICE. *Un peu.* I'm taking a French class twice a week. I love the language. (*Holding up a spoon.*) *La cuiller* ... (*Holding up a fork.*) *La forchette.* (*Holding up a napkin.*) *La serviette.* (*Holding up the menu.*) *Le menu.*

ELLIE. I knew that one.

ALICE. I think when you travel it's important to learn major words and phrases. I'm determined to not look like an idiot over there.

(*ELLIE hides behind a menu and starts to giggle. ALICE, too, looks through the menu. NED just stares at Ellie's menu. It begins to shake with laughter.*)

NED. Stop. Come on now, stop.

ELLIE. (*Coming out from behind the menu.*) *La cuiller ... la forchette ...*

NED. *Va t'en!*

ELLIE. Four years of French class and that's all you remember? *Tant pis.*

NED. *Va t'en!*

ELLIE. I think you're confusing your present conditional with your imperfect past ... Perhaps we should ask Alice?

NED. *Va t'en!*

ELLIE. (*Laughing.*) *"J'a faim."*

NED. *Va t'en!*

ELLIE. (*Sniffs the wine bottle.*) *"C'est magnifique!"*

NED. *Va t'en! Va t'en!*

ELLIE. (*Still laughing.*) Can't you just see her bouncing through the vineyards, *"Bonjour, Bonjour...* stomping grapes, sniffing bushes ...

NED. The French saying foul words back to her that she can't find in her Berlitz.

ELLIE. Her smiling back sweetly, *"Merci, merci."*

NED and ELLIE. (*Laughing.*) O-la-la.

(*THEY are both out of control. When they are finally able to catch their breath ...*)

ALICE. O-la-la. It all looks so good.

(*NED and ELLIE both lose it. NED "accidentally" knocks his fork onto the floor.*)

NED. Excuse me. (*HE goes under the table to catch his breath.*)

ELLIE. (*From behind the menu.*) *Excusez-moi!*

(*NED hits ELLIE from under the table. HE regains his composure and sits back up. ELLIE comes out from behind her menu.*)

ELLIE. You drop your *forchette?*

(*THEY both burst into laughter and BOTH go under the table. We hear MUSIC - A Gershwin ballad. After a moment, NED stands.*)

NED. Alice, before we order, would you care to dance?
ALICE. Sure. I guess.
ELLIE. Our restaurant ... Our table ... Our song.
ALICE. There doesn't seem to be anyone else on the dance floor.
NED. (*Shooting Ellie a glance.*) And there better not be.
ALICE. I'm not very good at this.
NED. We'll go slowly.

(*NED and ALICE dance around the room a bit. It appears to get romantic, then ...*)

ALICE. Did you know that the French produce over 60 million hectoliters of wine a year?

NED. I don't know that, no. We'll be sure to order another bottle.

ALICE. I'm glad I'm learning to speak French. Do you know what one of my dreams is?

NED. Tell dirty limericks to Armand Assante?

ALICE. *Pardon?*

NED. Nothing. What is your big dream?

ALICE. I want to read *La dame aux camélias* by Alexandre Dumas in the original French. Do you know the story?

NED. Not in the original French. I believe I know the original Hungarian.

ALICE. The novel opens with the sale of the personal effects of the notorious courtesan, Mademoiselle Marguerite Gautier in the Rue D'Antin. A gentleman purchases a copy of *Manon Lescaut,* and notices the inscription, *"Manon to Marguerite - Humilité!"* Humility. It was signed, Armand Duval. A few days later ...

(*As NED's eyes widen, ELLIE can contain herself no longer. SHE stands, crosses to the dancing couple, and taps ALICE on the shoulder.*)

ELLIE. *Pardonez-moi ...*

(*ELLIE cuts in and dances with NED. ALICE takes no notice of the switch at all. SHE dances alone chattering silently. Eventually, SHE moves into the shadows.*)

NED. Well ... tell me. What's the big news?

ELLIE. I'm going to be in a movie.

NED. (*A beat.*) What?

ELLIE. I got a movie.

NED. A movie? You're kidding? When? How?

ELLIE. I found out yesterday.

NED. Why didn't you call me? Do your folks know?

ELLIE. No. You're the first person I've told.

NED. Why aren't you screaming with joy? You're so calm. What's the matter?

ELLIE. Nothing's the matter.

NED. It's not a dirty movie, is it?

ELLIE. No!

NED. Then what is it?

ELLIE. I'm a little scared.

NED. You? Scared? (*HE dips her.*)

ELLIE. This is it. I mean, I think this could be it for me. It's a big part. The people in it are all big names ...

NED. What's the movie? What's it about?

ELLIE. I don't really want to talk about it. I haven't signed the contract yet, and I don't want to jinx it. But I had to tell you.

NED. I am so happy for you.

ELLIE. It's exciting. I can see things starting to come together.

NED. A movie star ... Parties ... Limousines ... Signing autographs.

ELLIE. Living in California for three short months ...

(*THEY stop dancing.*)

NED. Oh ... I didn't think about that.

ELLIE. (*A beat.*) You could come with me.

NED. I'll come out and visit, but I ... I've got things here. Too many things. Besides, you'll be back. You live here. You wanted to do Shakespeare in the park, and the park is here.

ELLIE. I almost didn't want to tell you. I knew this is the way you'd look.

NED. No, I'm elated. This is my elated look.

ELLIE. I wanted this evening to be a celebration.

NED. You're right. After all, you just got your first movie. We should be celebrating.

ELLIE. Neddie, don't worry. Everything will be just fine. Besides, I think it'll be good for us to be apart. Give you the chance to play the field.

NED. (*Pouting.*) I'll prolly never see you ever again.

ELLIE. Don't be silly. I'll be at the "ten year."

NED. Three months? What am I going to do while you're away for three months?

ELLIE. Water my plants. (*A beat.*) I'll be back, Ned. (*SHE kisses him.*)

NED. Things'll be pretty messy if you're not. We'll have to decide who gets custody of the restaurant, the table, the wine ...

ELLIE. What about *our* song?

NED. Joint custody. After all ... (*HE dips her, then dramatically ...*) We'll always have Berlin.

ELLIE. (*Still in the dip.*) It's Gershwin.

NED. Not my day.

ELLIE. If it was Berlin, that might've been funny.

NED. We can't have the stars and the moon, too.

ELLIE. Or something like that.

(*THEY kiss. The SONG ends. THEY turn to see ALICE float back onstage. SHE is still chattering silently to herself.*)

NED. What'll we do with Madame Du Barry?

ELLIE. She's not the right girl for you, Neddie. I think it's time for her to sail.

(*THEY both smile sweetly.*)

NED. Oh ... Alice ...

ALICE. (*Still floating.*) But you see Marguerite had left a journal for Duval so that he would know her dying thoughts were of him.

ELLIE. Try "*pardon.*"

NED. *Pardon*, Alice. *Pardon.*

(*ALICE coughs a few times a la Camille, then stops dancing and turns to Ned.*)

NED and ELLIE. Bon voyage!

(*ALICE stares at Ned, confused.*)

ALICE. *Bon soir.*

(*NED makes a foghorn noise. Both HE and ELLIE back away from Alice all the time waving goodbye. THEY exit.*)

ALICE. And then she dies ... all alone. Not knowing that he's loved her all these years. (*A beat then ...*) Ah ... *C'est magnifique!*

(*The LIGHTS fade out slowly and come up on RICK and NED sitting in the baseball stadium. RICK is eating popcorn. NED is looking through the binoculars.*)

RICK. You know, Ned Edwards, you are the most particular guy I know. I just don't get it. I mean, to not like a girl because she's got a beard ... or if she spits when she talks ... or if her father is a TV evangelist ... Those are girls I can see steering clear of. But Ned — to toss off a girl because she's on a diet or because she speaks a foreign language, don't you think you're getting a bit ... finicky?

(*NED looks at RICK but gives no response.*)

RICK. Ok. Ok. It's your ball game.

(*The LIGHTS change. NED disappears into the darkness and NORA appears on the other side of RICK. The ball park becomes a movie theatre. RICK is still eating popcorn. NORA is trying not to let Rick see how disgusted she is by the movie.*)

NORA. (*Whispering.*) I love it so far.
RICK. Wait, here comes the good part. This is great. Watch this.

(*THEY watch. A woman SCREAMS. NORA looks ill. RICK laughs.*)

RICK. Isn't this the best? I can hardly wait for this to come out on video tape.
NORA. Me too.
RICK. You know how we got that effect, don't you?
NORA. (*Whispering.*) No. Not really.
RICK. Jello brand instant Jello. A whole truck load of it. We mix it with baked beans — it gives that gloppy effect.
NORA. (*Whispering.*) It's remarkable.
RICK. (*Whispering.*) Why are you whispering?
NORA. (*Whispering.*) Because we're in a movie theatre.

RICK. But there's nobody else here. (*Shouting*.) Is anybody here? (*HE waits for a response. None.*) No one. There was a lady over there but she left.

NORA. I can't think why.

RICK. Some people don't like movies where young girls get into the shower, then get their flesh eaten away by baked beans.

NORA. How come ... whenever things get really scary, the girls decide to take a shower?

RICK. Well ...

NORA. I understand from a psychological point of view, that in the shower they would be at their most vulnerable.

RICK. That, and the fact that nobody would go see these pictures if the girls didn't get naked.

NORA. (*A beat.*) What did you do on this film?

RICK. I was the gaffer.

NORA. Really. (*A beat.*) What exactly does a gaffer do?

RICK. Oh, lots of technical things. You don't want to hear about that.

NORA. Yes. I do.

RICK. Don't you want to know which movie stars I've met?

NORA. (*A beat.*) No. I'd rather hear about being a gaffer.

(*RICK stares at Nora. The LIGHTS change back
    to NED and RICK at the game.*)

RICK. Have I got a girl for you.

NED. Not interested.

RICK. Wait till you see her.

NED. Another female wrestler? Or perhaps a friend of the Eskimo you fixed me up with. Or the gypsy palm reader? Or the cheerleader still in high school?

RICK. I swear I didn't know she was still in high school.

NED. The yarn wrapped around her school ring didn't tip you off?

RICK. I wasn't looking at the yarn wrapped around her ring. This woman is your type. I promise, Ned. Nice and quiet.

(*The LIGHTS switch back to NORA and RICK at the movie. NORA screams. RICK laughs.*)

RICK. I thought that might get you. Don't worry, that's not a real head. It's a cabbage with a wig. Say, Nora, I wanted to ask you ... Are you single?

NORA. (*Still recovering.*) Yes.

RICK. Not seeing anyone steady?

NORA. No.

RICK. That's great.

NORA. Rick, I think it's important for us to keep our relationship on a professional basis.

RICK. Oh, that's fine. I don't like you. But I have this friend ...

(*The LIGHTS on NED come up and he is included in the scene. All THREE stare out at the game/movie.*)

RICK. Her name is Nora. The only reason I'm passing her on and not keeping her for myself is she's your kind of nice, not mine.
NED. I don't know, Rick ...
NORA. You mean a blind date?
RICK. All I ask is that you give it a shot. (*To Nora.*) What do you say? (*To Ned.*) For me.
NED and NORA. I don't know.
RICK. I already said you'd go out together.
NED and NORA. You didn't?

(*RICK nods and waits for the verdict.*)

NED. All right.
NORA. When?

(*RICK smiles and climbs out of the seat leaving NED and NORA sitting together. HE turns back and pushes Ned closer to Nora. HE puts Ned's arm around her. RICK exits. NED and NORA sit, not too uncomfortably and watch the movie. Over the speakers we hear ELLIE's voice. "Funny running into you here ... After all this time. Isn't it just like us ..." Etc. NED's eyes widen in disbelief.*)

NED. Go away!

(*NORA looks at Ned. The LIGHTS fade to black. They come up on the loft. NORA is wandering around the loft, checking out Ned's books, etc.*)

NORA. Ned, I've had a wonderful evening. That restaurant was charming.
NED. (*Offstage.*) You liked it?
NORA. I did. I've never noticed it before.
NED. (*Offstage.*) It's been there for years. One of my favorites.
NORA. Now, it's one of mine.
NED. (*Enters with two glasses of port.*) I hope you like port. The perfect end to a perfect evening.
NORA. Oh, I do. But forgive me if I don't smoke a cigar with you.
NED. (*A beat.*) Do you smell cigars?
NORA. No. All I meant was ... port and cigars.
NED. Oh. (*Hands her the glass.*)
NORA. Thanks.
NED. (*Toasting.*) To our friend, Rick.
NORA. And to all the movie stars he's met.
NED. Oh, he gave you his list, did he?

(*NORA nods.*)

NED. You obviously weren't impressed or you'd be out with him tonight.
NORA. Things like that don't impress me.

NED. Well, then I won't give you my list.

NORA. This is quite good. So thick.

NED. It's like really good cough syrup.

NORA. That wine tonight was good also.

NED. It didn't bother you that it was served in a burgundy glass?

NORA. You noticed that too, did you? No. It didn't bother me at all.

NED. Glad to hear it. (*A beat.*) May I take this moment to tell you how refreshing it is to meet you.

NORA. Please do.

NED. It's been a terrific evening.

NORA. It has. Although, I must admit, it was a touch and go there during the movie.

NED. You didn't like it? (*HE downs the port.*) Oh, I didn't think the movie was that bad. (*Exits to the kitchen.*)

NORA. You didn't? (*Wanders around the loft, looking at Ned's photographs, books, his portfolios, etc.*)

NED. (*Offstage.*) Perhaps a little bloody. The nudity completely gratuitous.

NORA. However did you find that out? ... You left soon after the opening credits and didn't return until the closing ones.

(*After a moment, NED pokes his head into the room.*)

NED. There was this incredibly long line at the popcorn concession.

(*NORA smiles.*)

NED. Incredibly long.

(*NED exits. NORA finds a picture of Ellie tucked away in one of Ned's portfolios.*)

NORA. It bothers you to see her up on the screen?
NED. (*Enters with the decanter.*) Who?
NORA. Her. (*SHE holds up the photograph.*) The reason for that incredibly long line.
NED. (*Smiling.*) However did that escape the incinerator? (*A beat.*) I'm sorry I disappeared on you. It wasn't a very nice thing to do. Were you angry?
NORA. No. But there were moments when I was curious.
NED. Another strange blind date, huh?
NORA. I've had my share. But fortunately, you redeemed yourself during dinner. You didn't disappear once.

(*NORA turns to see that NED has disappeared once more to remove the portfolio.*)

NORA. (*Calling off.*) I take it you don't keep in touch?

NED. (*Offstage.*) No. Not at all.
NORA. And you never see her ... Just to talk?
NED. (*Offstage.*) See her? I don't even think about her.

(*A pause. ELLIE pokes her head into the room, then makes herself comfortable on the couch.*)

NORA. How long ago did you break up?

NED. (*Reenters.*) Oh, it's been a long time. (*HE sees Ellie.*) How long has it been? (*NED clears the rest of the table. HE picks up a large tray of slides.*)
ELLIE. Little over two years.
NED. (*To Nora.*) Little over two ...

(*HE realizes Ellie's back. HE turns to see her, and the slides go all over the floor. SHE gives him a little smile and a wave.*)

NED. Ahh!
NORA. I'm sorry. I didn't mean to bring back old memories.
NED. *You* haven't.
NORA. Must have been a pretty serious relationship.
NED. Just a long one. I've known her since we were fourteen. (*Begins picking up slides.*)
NORA. And you don't keep in touch?
NED. Why all this interest in Eleanor?

NORA. I'm sorry. I just think you can learn a lot about people by seeing who they're attracted to. Don't you agree?

(NORA sits on the floor with NED and helps him pick up the slides. ELLIE sits on the back of the couch to get a better view.)

ELLIE. I think I liked the wino better.

NORA. All I'm saying, is that I'm fascinated by seeing who peoples' friends are. What books they read. What movies they like. You have to admit that your photography must reveal what kind of person you are.

ELLIE. "He keeps his shoes in pairs but not in a row." What a snoop! Let's move on, Ned. We can do better than this. *(Calling out.)* Next.

NED. *(To Nora.)* I agree with you completely.

NORA. You said earlier this evening, that you won't take a permanent job working at that advertising agency. That tells me something about you. It says you're not the type to sell out.

NED. Well, it's not that. I photograph the shots I do, because it's the only way I know how to photograph.

(ELLIE has heard it before. SHE disappears behind the couch.)

NORA. It's not *what* you see, but *how* you see it.

NED. Exactly. (*Picks a slide up off the floor.*) Like this, for example. If you were driving down this dirt road, you'd probably never notice this turn-of-the-century gazebo. On one side was this burnt out farmhouse. Not far from it was a bulldozer ready to clear the way for the future. (*A beat.*) If I was working for the advertising folk, they would like a shot of the gazebo – but make it look pretty. Better yet, build a new one in a studio. (*An idea – another slide.*) For *Life* magazine, how about a shot of the bulldozer attacking not the burnt out farmhouse, but the gazebo? You know, destroying the past. Very artistic. Award winning photo.

NORA. And what did you see?

(*NED hands Nora the slide. ELLIE's head pops up.*)

NED. If you look up gazebo in the dictionary it means ...

(*ELLIE mouths it with him.*)

NED. "I shall gaze."

(*ELLIE yawns and disappears behind the couch.*)

NED. So, with my tools of the trade, I blocked out the bulldozer and the farmhouse, and placed this antique pavilion in the distance – alone on this bluff, as it has stood for probably a hundred years. Maybe it will stand a hundred more or maybe only another week. But here, as I see it — it shall gaze forever. An elegant reminder of a much more civilized time when we built homes strictly to appreciate the view. (*A beat.*) So I agree with you. My photography does reveal what kind of person I am.

(*Silence, then ... ELLIE comes out from behind the couch.*)

ELLIE. My God, I thought you'd never get to the point.
NORA. I like it.
NED. I'm what you'd call a "wet belly photographer."
NORA. And what's that?
ELLIE. Don't encourage him.
NED. I'd prefer lying for hours on a cold, wet beach in February to catch the waves break, than sitting in a warm, dry studio shooting baby pictures. Or worse, teaching all about it at the New School.
NORA. You're very talented.
NED. Well, enough about me. We've spent too much time talking about my life and loves. What about you? You were hesitant earlier to tell me what you did. You work for KGB?
NORA. I'm a teacher at the New School.
NED. You're kidding?

(HE laughs. SHE laughs.)

NORA. Yes. I am.
ELLIE. She's a regular comic. *(Facetiously.)* Jump on this women, Ned. Don't let her out the door.

(NED kisses Nora.)

ELLIE. I didn't mean for you to take me seriously. Ned? Ned? Stop that, Ned.

(NED and NORA are still entwined.)

ELLIE. I just hate it when you're *not* "not concentrating."
NORA. Actually, I'm a therapist.
ELLIE. No. Go on. You? A therapist?
NORA. I'm always leery of telling people. They either get frightened or pour their hearts out.
ELLIE. *(To Ned.)* You did both.
NED. I suppose you get off on analyzing idealistic photographers?
NORA. If I have a choice, I prefer "wet bellied" ones.
ELLIE. This is disgusting. I'm leaving.
NED. *(To both.)* I don't think you have a choice.

(THEY kiss again.)

NORA. You were wrong in thinking that port was the end to a perfect evening.

(*NED and NORA head towards the bedroom.*)

ELLIE. Ned Edwards. Come back here.
NED. (*Stops. To Nora.*) You go ahead. I'll be right there.
NORA. You're not a little nervous, are you, Ned?
NED. Now, don't start analyzing.
NORA. Sorry. Force of habit. I promise, if I ask questions, you can snap photographs.
NED. Deal.

(*NORA exits. NED watches her go. Then ...*)

NED. What?
ELLIE. I don't like her, Ned.

(*NED angrily picks up the rest of the slides off the floor.*)

NED. I don't care.
ELLIE. She's too put together. (*Her imitation.*) "If I ask questions, you can snap photographs ..."
NED. Well, I like her. She's pretty, she's smart, she's funny ... she likes what I do, more than that, she understands what I do. (*A beat.*) Go away, Ellie. I don't want to see you anymore. I

don't want you hanging around. I've found someone who I care about, and I don't want you getting in the way. Please, leave me alone!

(*NED exits. ELLIE sits silently trying not to show any emotion. The LIGHTS begin to fade.*)

ELLIE. (*Whispering after him.*) See ya at the "ten year."

(*ELLIE counts to ten on her fingers. Just before the room is dark, the LIGHTS stop fading and begin to fade back up. Before she reaches ten, a smile forms on ELLIE's lips. SHE's been summoned. SHE stands, and exits to the bedroom in triumph. BLACKOUT.*)

END OF ACT I

ACT II

CANDLES light the loft. The couch has been pushed to the side of the room. NED and ELLIE are dancing to a Gershwin ballad. NED is wearing a smoking jacket and sweat pants. ELLIE is in a flowing robe. After several spins around the room ...

ELLIE. Shall we throw another log on the fire?

NED. You weren't thinking of making anymore of these silly things, were you?

ELLIE. Films. Nah. It's time, I feel, to develop our natural talent for ballroom dancing.

NED. You think that, do you?

ELLIE. I do. I really do.

NED. Blame it all on that Halloween party we went to dressed as ...

ELLIE. Vernon and Irene Castle.

NED. Everyone stared.

ELLIE. Well that's only natural, don't you think?

NED. I do.

ELLIE. We're the only two people ...

NED. Under eighty ...

ELLIE. That know who they were.

NED. (*A thought.*) Shall we do it?
ELLIE. I beg your pardon?
NED. Shall we have a go at it? The topper?
ELLIE. The topper? You think we dare?
NED. I do. I really do.
ELLIE. (*Announcing it.*) The topper!
NED. The topper!

(*THEY finish the dance by stepping up on the couch trying to send it over on its back.*)

ELLIE. (*Laughing.*) No wait ... I wasn't mentally prepared.
NED. Cut! Take two. Come on Irene, let's try it again.
ELLIE. (*Announcing it.*) The topper!
NED. The topper!

(*Again, THEY're unable to send the couch over on its back.*)

NED. Not tonight, Irene.
ELLIE. Shall we cheat?
NED. I think it best.

(*THEY check to see that no one is watching, and slyly push the couch over on its back.*)

ELLIE. If memory serves ... I do believe that *I* was dressed as Vernon Castle.

NED. Correct me if I'm wrong ... I'm almost positive it was *I*, who went as Vernon.

ELLIE. (*A beat.*) Do you mean to say ...

NED. (*Realizing.*) We both went to the party dressed as ...

NED and ELLIE. Vernon Castle!

NED. (*A beat.*) No wonder they all stared.

ELLIE. You silly man, you.

(*With as much grace as they can muster, THEY fall back onto the over-turned couch. Finally...*)

ELLIE. Neddie ...

NED. Whatie?

ELLIE. It's good to be back.

NED. God, I missed you.

ELLIE. I missed you, too.

NED. I hope you never go away for half a year again.

ELLIE. It was not half a year. It was five and a half months.

NED. It was supposed to be three.

ELLIE. I know. But I got paid for an extra two and a half months.

NED. Oh, well that's different.

ELLIE. Ned, I love doing films.

NED. Films? You've only done one.

ELLIE. They're much more difficult than you would think.

(*Throughout this speech, NED just watches, listens and smiles.*)

ELLIE. Like my first day, we shot my final scene where my husband tells me he's leaving me, and I burst into tears. We were in this restaurant and there're all these people around. Well, Neddie, I didn't know if I could do it. I mean, my first day on the set, and I had to cry. The director said I could always use glycerin. They squirt it in your eyes. Well, Bobbie ... his friends all call him Bobbie — he's so sweet — comes up to me and tells me not to sweat it. He knows I can do it. More pressure. But, Neddie ... when the camera started rolling, and Bobbie says he's leaving — I cried. I really cried. Do you believe it? I can cry on cue. Everyone applauded after the scene. It was the neatest thing.

(*NED just stares at her, smiles, then applauds.*)

ELLIE. Feel free to stop me if I babble.
NED. (*Holds out an imaginary microphone.*) Tell me, when the tears began welling up, were you thinking about your dead dog or anything?
ELLIE. (*Playing along.*) Sparky? No. At first, I tried to think about all the world's problems, but ... but ...
NED. But you couldn't think of any.
ELLIE. Well, not that fast. But finally I thought ... "Elvis," and I cried.

NED. Amazing. Can't wait to see the flick. We just know you'll be dazzling. That's all from Hollywoodland.

(*THEY stare at each other a moment.*)

ELLIE. Go ahead, laugh.

NED. Tell us more Bobbie stories.

ELLIE. No. I'm through. What about you? What have you been up to?

NED. Oh, this and that. I've been busy. Nothing worth crying over.

ELLIE. (*Looks at him, refusing to laugh.*) Well, I have news.

NED. You can yawn on cue.

ELLIE. I am never telling you another thing as long as I live.

NED. I'm sorry.

ELLIE. No ... never.

NED. I said I'm sorry. Come on. Tell me your news. You've been cast in a Broadway show?

ELLIE. Yes.

NED. You're kidding?

ELLIE. Nope. Found out yesterday.

NED. You really are telling the truth?

ELLIE. Yes. A musical. It sounds a little strange, but I don't care. It's coming to Broadway.

NED. When?

ELLIE. The fall. We tour for the summer, a week in St. Louis, Baltimore, I forget where, and then we come into New York. About the time the movie is supposed to come out. November. Wouldn't it be funny it it all happened on my birthday?

NED. I'd only have to get one card.

(*Silence.*)

ELLIE. I was afraid to tell you. It's only for the summer.

NED. November?

ELLIE. Well, I'm not going to turn it down.

NED. I'm not saying you should. I think it's great. And hell, it's Broadway. Congratulations.

ELLIE. Thank you, Ned.

NED. This sort of makes me want to ask you something that I've been sort of thinking about these last few months.

ELLIE. Neddie, don't. Please don't.

NED. Why not?

ELLIE. This just isn't the right time. There's too much going on.

NED. Not for me. All I do is write letters. I don't see what difference it makes. All I know is that while I'm writing, I would feel differently.

(*Silence. ELLIE leans over and kisses him.*)

ELLIE. Thanks anyway. (*Silence.*) We'll always be together. We have to be. We're so much alike. (*A beat.*) I remember the day we met in sophomore English. You sat in that class for an entire year and never said a word. (*As ELLIE tells the story, she cannot control her laughter.*) Not a word. And the last day of class, you raised your hand. The entire class was in shock. We have never heard your voice. And you said with such conviction, "Edna St. Vincent Millay!" And then the bell rang.

NED. (*Begins to laugh, too.*) It was the answer to the question.

ELLIE. Neddie, the question was asked on the first day of class. It took a year for you to answer that question.

NED. As I recall, it was a difficult question.

ELLIE. For a whole year, you sat there in silence and planned what you would say on the last day. "Edna St. Vincent Millay!" Everyone just stared at you. Nobody got it.

NED. Except you. You're the only one who gets my jokes.

ELLIE. That is so sweet.

NED. Sorta makes you want to cry, doesn't it?

(*A pause. NED glances towards Ellie to see if she's crying.*)

ELLIE. What are you ... (*SHE gets it.*)
NED. That was your cue, and you blew it.
ELLIE. You ass. (*SHE hits him with a pillow.*)
NED. I guess you'll have to use the glycerin.

(*SHE hits him again.*)

NED. Bobbie will be so disappointed.

ELLIE. Neddie Edwards, I am not going to play with you anymore.

NED. That's what I'm afraid of.

(*Long pause.*)

ELLIE. Neddie, don't be mad at me. You are very special to me. But I just can't. Not now. (*Quickly.*) I've got a swell idea. What do you say we play a game?

NED. Now?

ELLIE. What's wrong with now?

NED. It must be at least four in the morning.

ELLIE. At least.

NED. (*A beat.*) Hey, why not? But first ... (*NED stands, and helps ELLIE up. HE puts the couch back on its feet.*) What do you say we have another go at ... the topper?

ELLIE. Do you think we dare?

NED. I do. I really do.

ELLIE. (*Announcing it.*) The topper!

NED. The topper!

(*THEY very gracefully step up on the couch. Then up on the back of the couch, flipping it over. THEY both fall gently back down onto the couch and laugh hysterically. NORA enters from the bedroom. SHE is wearing a nightgown.*)

NORA. Ned?

ELLIE. What is she doing here? What is this? A slumber party?

NED. Nora, what are you doing up so late?

NORA. It was a little hard to sleep with you laughing. What's so funny? Why are you sitting here with all these candles lit? You're not into some kind of religious cult, are you?

NED. No.

NORA. Are you all right?

(*NED blows out the candles.*)

ELLIE. How come after you start seeing someone for a few months they begin asking you if you're feeling all right?

NED. I'm fine. I couldn't sleep. I'm just sitting here – daydreaming.

NORA. It's four o'clock in the morning. At *night*, you're supposed to daydream while you're *asleep*.

ELLIE. There she goes analyzing again.

NED. I guess I don't do it the right way. Ignore me.

NORA. It's a little hard to ignore a laughing man at four in the morning.

(*NED looks at Ellie.*)

ELLIE. I'm not going to touch it. Not my kind of humor.

NED. (*To Nora.*) I'm sorry.

NORA. Ned, is it us?

NED. Us? No.

ELLIE. Here we go.

NORA. Something I'm puzzled by ... (*SHE notices the couch.*) What happened to the couch?

ELLIE. We put it out of its misery.

(*NED smiles. After a moment ...*)

ELLIE. I've got a swell idea ...

NED. (*Immediately.*) I've got a swell idea ...

ELLIE. What do you say we play a game?

NED. What do you say we play a game?

NORA. Now?

NED. (*To Ellie.*) Now?

ELLIE. What's wrong with now?

NED. (*To Nora.*) What's wrong with now?

NORA. It must be four o'clock in the morning.

ELLIE. At least.

NED. (*To Nora.*) At least. (*A beat, then to Ellie.*) Hey, why not?

ELLIE. I remember your response. I want to hear what she says.

(*Silence. NED and ELLIE turn to Nora.*)

NORA. *Why* do you want to play a game?

ELLIE. (*To Nora.*) Because it's a test. Don't you get it?

NORA. You want to play ... a game ... in the middle of the night?

NED and ELLIE. Yes.

(*Silence.*)

NORA. Hey, why not?

ELLIE. Damn it.

NORA. I'm wide awake; we might as well.

NED. (*Looking at Ellie, but responding to Nora.*) Good. I'm glad. This will be fun. You'll love this game.

ELLIE. I go first.

NED. You always go first.

NORA. I've never even played with you. How could I always go first?

NED. Right.

ELLIE. Steady does it buster. She'll have you in a straight jacket so fast ...

NED. (*To Ellie.*) Sorry.

ELLIE. All right. You go first. But don't do something too bizarre. Pick something I know.

NED. I'll go first. It's sort of like charades. Only there's music ...

ELLIE. And costumes.

NED. And costumes. (*Exits.*)

NORA. Costumes?

NED. (*Offstage.*) It'll be fun. I promise.

(*A silence. The two women sit together on the over-turned couch.*)

ELLIE. You know, if you had said no to the game, you'd be outta here and Neddie and I would be back together. By playing along, you're only leading him on.

(*No response from NORA.*)

ELLIE. Tell me, how can you wear that to bed? Doesn't it creep up on you?

(*We hear MUSIC.*)

ELLIE. I don't recognize this music.

(*A moment later NED enters, wearing his bedspread.*)

ELLIE. You're Jesus. It's a movie. "The Robe."

(*NED gives her a look.*)

ELLIE. No, huh?

(*HE wraps the bedspread around his head.*)

ELLIE. Sandra Dee. "Tammy and the Doctor." (*Another look.*) Just kidding. Let's see ... you're an Arab?

(*NED nods, yes.*)

ELLIE. Lawrence of Arabia.

(*NED shakes his head, no.*)

ELLIE. I don't know any Arabs. I've got it ... "The Desert Song?"

(*No. A pause.*)

NORA. I'm not very good at games. Are you some kind of religious figure? Jesus, perhaps?

(*NED shakes his head, no.*)

ELLIE. Where have you been?
NORA. Moses?

(*NED moves his lips in a sensuous way, but does not talk out loud.*)

NORA. Mary Magdeline?

(*No!*)

ELLIE. A silent movie?

NORA. John the Baptist?

(*A nod yes, then a no.*)

ELLIE. Well, which is it? Yes, or no?
NED. (*To Ellie.*) Yes, to you. No, to her.
ELLIE. You're not supposed to talk.

(*NED goes back to mouthing words.*)

ELLIE. All right. It's a movie. A silent movie.

(*NED shows us that he's illustrating the whole picture.*)

ELLIE. You're acting out the whole silent movie.
NORA. I've got it.

(*Silence.*)

NORA. You're feeding the 5000 with one loaf of bread.

(*Looks from BOTH of them.*)

NORA. I didn't think so.
ELLIE. You're Chaplin ... Keaton ...
NORA. Luke ... John ...

(*No.*)

ELLIE. Any movie with Mary Pickford in it?

(*NED turns around and mimes hugging
    himself.*)

ELLIE. You're a lover?

(*Nod, yes.*)

ELLIE. A famous lover?
NORA. Mary Magdeline?
NED and ELLIE. (*To Nora.*) No!

(*NED gets an idea. HE runs offstage.*)

NORA. Are you one of the twelve disciples?
Let's see, there's James ... Simon, who was called
Peter. What was Peter's brother's name?
    ELLIE. (*Helping out.*) Dopey ... Sleepy ...
Grumpy ...
    NED. (*Offstage, to Ellie.*) Stop!

(*The MUSIC becomes recognizable. It is "The
    Sheik of Araby."*)

ELLIE. I know this music. Wait, I'll get this.

(*NED reenters. HE has the bedspread tied around
    his head. HE strikes a dramatic pose.*)

ELLIE. Rudolph Valentino! You're Rudolph Valentino!

(*NED nods, yes.*)

ELLIE. But that's not the answer. You're Rudolph Valentino in some movie.

(*NED pulls Ellie into the movie. HE starts making love to her like Valentino, very dramatically, all the while still talking with no sound.*)

ELLIE. I don't know any Valentino movies.

(*NED lowers her to the ground.*)

ELLIE. They're never on TV.

(*HE kisses her.*)

ELLIE. Now I know why.
NORA. Kissing ...
ELLIE. (*A beat.*) If she says Mary Magdeline again ...
NORA. Judas Iscariot?
ELLIE. (*Pushes Ned back.*) Wait. I know it. "The Sheik." Am I right? It's "The Sheik." I'm right, aren't I?
NED. No.

ELLIE. No?

(*NED shakes his head, no.*)

NORA. No, huh? I thought for sure you were Judas.
NED. It's not "The Sheik."
ELLIE. I don't know then. I give up. What is it?
NED. (*Smile.*) "Son of the Sheik."
ELLIE. More like son of a ...
NED. Shhh ... It's a silent movie.

(*THEY kiss. Finally ...*)

ELLIE. My turn. I'm going to do a movie, too.
NED. (*Still kissing her.*) Let's forget your movie ... and stay in mine.

(*THEY do. Finally ...*)

NORA. Wait ... Stop ... I know what's going on. I've figured you out, Ned Edwards. You're not alone.

(*THEY stop kissing and turn to Nora.*)

NORA. It's "The Last Supper," isn't it?

(*NED falls back onto the floor – giving up the game. After a moment, HE starts laughing. NORA joins in.*)

NED. "The Last Supper?"
NORA. No, huh?
NED. How, with all the kissing and passion I was trying to exude, did you ever come up with "The Last Supper?"
NORA. I told you I wasn't very good at games.
NED. That's true. You did. But "The Last Supper?"

(*THEY both laugh. Then ...*)

NED. Come on, let's go back to sleep.
NORA. Aren't you going to tell me what you were doing?
ELLIE. Don't tell her, Ned. It'll drive her crazy.
NORA. Come on, give me another chance.
NED. (*Puts his arm around Nora.*) All right. One more chance. Only this time, no music and no costumes.

(*THEY both head off to the bedroom. ELLIE watches.*)

ELLIE. Hey! Rudy! Remember me? I won the game.

(*As NED and NORA are exiting, NED holds out his other arm. ELLIE runs over to them, and all three disappear behind the bedspread and exit. The LIGHTS fade and come up on RICK lying on the couch with the VCR remote in his hand. HE is watching a tape of one of his movies.*)

RICK. (*Calling offstage to Ned.*) It's ok. You don't have to thank me.

NED. (*Offstage.*) For what?

RICK. For introducing you to the girl of your dreams.

(*NED enters with several boxes of slides. HE sits at the light box and edits.*)

NED. Do we have to watch this?

RICK. I love to watch this stuff on tape. You can speed through the plot.

NED. It amazes me that she knows that there is this flesh sucking, mucousy, baked-beaned looking alien on the loose, and so what does she decide to do?

RICK. Take a shower.

NED. No wonder you're in therapy. Is Nora helping you at all?

RICK. Too soon to tell. How're you guys doing?

NED. Too soon to tell. (*A beat.*) You see, I've been seeing someone else as well.

RICK. What? You're dating another girl, too?

NED. Not dating. Seeing.

RICK. Huh?

NED. I'm *seeing* another girl. I'm dating Nora. But I can't help *seeing someone else.*

RICK. There's nothing wrong with that. You and Nora aren't married or anything. Who is she? The other girl.

NED. It's difficult to explain.

RICK. All the fixing up I've done, and you found someone on your own. Who is she?

NED. Ellie.

RICK. Ellie! You're seeing Ellie again?

NED. I can't seem to get her out of my mind. Especially when I'm with another girl.

RICK. You're seeing Ellie?

NED. Except that Ellie isn't really there.

RICK. Huh?

NED. She sort of visits me in my head. Says things that Ellie would say. It's like she's haunting me.

RICK. Haunting you? She's not there?

NED. No.

RICK. You mean to tell me you're cheating on your girlfriend — in spirit?

NED. I never said I was proud of it. I thought for sure Ellie would be history when Nora came along. I really like Nora.

RICK. So what's the problem?

NED. I feel like I'm dating my therapist.

RICK. No, you're dating *my* therapist.

NED. We have fun. We enjoy hearing about what each other does. We have similar interests. We both love your movies. It all seems so comfortable.

RICK. What do you want to do, knock over furniture?

NED. Yes, actually. Nora is so pleasant. So agreeable.

RICK. I hate that in a woman.

NED. I want a girl who's not going to let me get away with things. Catch me ... Give me grief...

RICK. They're hard to find.

NED. I know from past experience that it gets better than this. What do I do?

RICK. (*A beat.*) Watch the movie.

(*RICK flips around on the couch. The LIGHTS come up on NORA. THEY are in the middle of his therapy session.*)

RICK. When I was 8 or 9, my father brought home a Mickey Mouse sprinkler for the back yard. The little neighbor girl and I used to put on our swim suits, and run under the water on hot summer days. When her family moved, I never went under again. Weird, huh?

NORA. (*A beat.*) Does he talk to you about her?

RICK. Who? My father ... or Mickey?

NORA. Ned.

RICK. Ned?

NORA. Ned. I can't get him to talk about her.

RICK. You think the sprinkler means anything?

NORA. (*A beat.*) Sprinkler?

(*RICK turns back to Ned. The LIGHTS change.*)

RICK. Have you discussed seeing Ellie with Nora?

NED. Are you kidding? She'd only put it under the microscope. Besides, I'm trying not to think of Ellie. I don't like talking about her. I don't want to be reminded of her. Most guys break up with a girl and they never see her again. They're lucky. I've tried to avoid mine every night this week on a mini series.

RICK. Did you see her interviewed on TV this morning?

NED. No, I missed that. What a shame. Fortunately, I have my family and friends to keep me posted. My mother sends me clippings, you keep trying to drag me to the movies ...

RICK. How does that make you feel?

NED. Huh?

RICK. Ned, you mad because she's doing so well?

NED. No, not at all. (*Sincerely.*) I'm thrilled for her. She wanted this career so badly. (*A beat.*) I just wish she was having it in Australia.

RICK. Jealous.

NED. No. I'm not jealous. I just can't stand to know that she's doing it, and I can't be there to share it with her.

(*Silence. The LIGHTS on Ned fade and come back up on NORA.*)

NORA. Then last week I catch him kissing a pillow on the couch.
RICK. How does that make you feel?

(*The LIGHTS switch back to Ned.*)

NED. We were walking down Amsterdam one afternoon, and this pay phone on the street just started ringing. No one was around. We both stopped, turned our heads toward the phone, and Ellie, with the most blasé attitude, turned to me and said, "I left this number." Or maybe I said it. I don't remember. But we both laughed. Things always happened to us that we found just hysterical. Nora and I don't have that.

(*The LIGHTS come up on NORA.*)

NORA. A couple of weeks ago we leave this party and he turns to me and asks, "What do you think of Irving Berlin?" I said, "I think he has a massive inferiority complex." Ned just stares at me. I thought he was referring to this little

German guy with horned-rim glasses we met at the party.

NED. (*To Rick.*) I said, "Don't you think his music is romantic?" And you know what she said?

(*RICK turns to Nora to see if she'll tell him. No. HE turns back to Ned.*)

NED. She says, "I don't think *God Bless America* is romantic.

NORA. Patriotic, yes.

NED. It just isn't there.

NORA. Let's face it, I don't need to compete with a movie star.

NED. It's like there's something missing, but I ...

NORA. Don't know what it is.

NED. What do I do?

NORA. Am I overreacting?

NED. Do you think she needs to be a little more tolerant?

NORA. (*Overlapping with Ned.*) I couldn't be more tolerant.

NED. What do you think, Rick?

NORA. Rick ...

NED. Say something ...

RICK. (*Thinks it over. Finally ...*) That's all we'll have time for today.

(*BLACKOUT. The LIGHTS come up on an upstage scrim. Behind it is ELLIE, her foot up on a small stool. SHE is performing the role of Charlotta in "The Cherry Orchard." SHE is in costume and is adjusting the strap on a rifle. ELLIE has improved since we last saw her perform.*)

ELLIE. (*Pensively.*) When I was a little girl, my father and mother used to travel with the fair. They gave performances, very good ones. And I would do the "salto mortale" and all sorts of tricks. And when Papa and Mama died, a German lady took me to live with her and gave me lessons. When I grew up, I became a governess. But where I come from, and who I am, I don't know. Or who my parents were – perhaps they weren't even married ... I don't know. (*SHE takes a cucumber out of her pocket, snaps it in two and eats it.*) I know nothing at all. I'd like so much to talk, but there's not anyone. I haven't anyone.

(*The LIGHTS fade on ELLIE and a red LIGHT comes up on RICK and NED in the darkroom. NED is busy developing a photo. RICK sits on a stool drinking his beer.*)

RICK. God, it's dark in here.
NED. That's the general idea.

RICK. Kinda spooky, too. (*HE makes scary noises.*) If it didn't smell so bad, it's be a great place to bring girls.

NED. Here it is. (*Hands Rick a photograph.*)

RICK. This isn't anything new. I've seen this before.

NED. I'm trying to illustrate something.

RICK. I'm sitting in the dark on a sunny Saturday afternoon so you can play Mr. Science?

NED. When I'm finished, everything will be clear.

RICK. What am I confused about?

NED. You see ... you don't even know. That's why we're doing this. (*A beat.*) Now ... This photograph is a double exposure.

RICK. You were right. I didn't know that. That is amazing. Wow! Now, can we get out of here and have some fun?

NED. Shut up. Drink your beer. This is fun. First, let's start with the island ...

(*NED puts a photograph into his solution. Behind the upstage scrim, an island complete with palm tree appears in silhouette. RICK turns upstage and sees it.*)

RICK. I wish I was there now.

NED. No, you don't. The day I took that photograph it was about 110 degrees out. And humid. You couldn't even breathe.

(*ELLIE enters and leans on the tree.*)

NED. Now we add the girl.
RICK. Well, its about time. Is that Ellie?
NED. Yeah. I shot her in silhouette.
RICK. She looks great. Is she naked?
NED. If it will make you happy, then yes.
RICK. It does. Thank you.
NED. She was also being eaten alive by the mosquitoes.

(*ELLIE in silhouette, starts slapping at the bugs.*)

NED. If I had used a telephoto, you would have seen this blotchy, bitten, very angry girl.

(*The BACKLIGHT changes to FRONT LIGHT for a moment, so that we can see Ellie's true feelings.*)

NED. It was a tough shot to get, too. I was out in this row boat. Took me over an hour to row out and back. I got a pretty nasty sunburn.
RICK. You got a sunburn at night? God, you are a sensitive kinda guy.
NED. I didn't shoot at night. I couldn't have gotten the silhouettes I wanted, so I shot in the day and filtered out most of the light.
RICK. And when you do that, the moon appears. Thank you, Mr. Science.

NED. No, it doesn't. (*Pleased with himself.*) This is the fun part. There was no moon that night.

RICK. This is sort of like a mystery. (*HE makes his scary noises again.*) This place is perfect. You got to get a shower installed in here, Ned. Trust me.

NED. First thing in the morning.

RICK. Ok, ok, I give ... If there was no moon that night ...

NED. (*Puts another photo into the solution.*) I added the moon.

(*The MOON appears.*)

RICK. *You* added the moon!

NED. I shot that moon a couple of months later.

RICK. That's *your* moon?

NED. A 200mm lens makes it that large. Neat, huh?

RICK. *You* added your own big moon!

NED. If you shoot it when it's closest to us, the pollution gives it that orange color.

RICK. You added your own big, dirty moon!

NED. I wanted a moon. There wasn't one. So I superimposed one onto my photograph. I barely got that shot before Ellie jumped into the water to escape the mosquitos.

(*SHE does so. The "photograph" disappears.*)

RICK. Was the tree fake, too?

NED. No, the tree was not fake. I did add a few palm leaves. More sand ...

RICK. You're disillusioning me, Ned.

NED. I didn't think that was possible.

RICK. I work in the movies. I know that the work I do is ...

NED. Full of beans?

RICK. Yes. Thank you. But you, Ned? You, a guy who still believes in the Easter bunny ... You, resorting to trickery?

NED. Ellie used to say that both actors and photographers create illusions to trick our viewers into feeling what we want them to.

RICK. So that's why you dragged me in here on my day off? To tell me you're a fake?

NED. No, it's not. And I'm not a fake. It isn't phony to me. I'm not trying to trick you. No matter what this place was really like, with the heat, the bugs, the lizards ...

RICK. There were lizards?

NED. On that particular weekend, for the two of us — the moon was out!

RICK. You dog!

NED. That's why I had to add it. Memory adds moonlight. (*A beat.*) Now do you get it?

RICK. Well, of course. (*HE doesn't at all.*)

NED. When I'm with Nora the moon isn't out.

(*The island reappears. NORA in silhouette. SHE is wearing a cute sundress and sun hat. SHE waves, grabs the palm tree, and exits.*)

RICK. You can't superimpose a moon? Even a little one?

NED. Believe me, I've tried. (*A beat.*) Am I too fussy? Do I want too much?

RICK. Nah. But if I were you Ned, I'd think twice about throwing over a real girl for a dream.

NED. All the unique girls I've been out with and then Nora comes along. And she's terrific. And I'm a lucky guy to know her. But something isn't right.

RICK. Ellie wasn't perfect.

NED. No. *Nora* is the perfect girl. She's the best. But I still miss Ellie. At times, I wish I could take the best of both girls, and roll them in a ball, throw them up in the air and see what lands.

RICK. It sounds good. But, I know from personal experience that girls don't seem to care for it.

NED. I want being with Nora to be the way it was with Ellie.

RICK. Sounds like your trying to superimpose Ellie onto Nora.

NED. (*A pause.*) I have a feeling that this therapy stuff is creating a monster.

RICK. Ned, this has nothing to do with photography. Nothing to do with big moons, tropical islands, or Nora. (*A beat.*) You're still in love with Ellie.

NED. I am not. That's all over years ago. (*NED grabs his darkroom equipment and exits. The LIGHTS come up and we are in the loft.*)

RICK. Liar

NED. (*Offstage.*) It is.

RICK. Liar, liar.

NED. (*Reenters with his beer.*) Just because I think about her does not mean I want to get back together. Ellie didn't want the same things I wanted out of the relationship. I have a tendency to remember only the moonlight. But that's ages ago. I'm not still in love with her.

RICK. Liar. (*A pause.*) Why don't you give her a call?

NED. What?

RICK. Call her up. Just to talk.

NED. I'm not calling her up. No way.

RICK. She hasn't called you?

NED. She'll never call me. And I'll never call her. We're both too stubborn.

RICK. Neddie, stop being such an ass, and call her. If you still feel so strongly about her, then bend just a little, and call her.

NED. I don't feel strongly.

RICK. Ha, ha! Then why are we arguing about her?

NED. I hate it when you do this. I absolutely hate it. Besides, I vowed never to call her.

RICK. Well, we wouldn't want you to break a vow. (*A beat.*) You mean to tell me that in the last two years you haven't seen or talked to her once?

NED. No.

RICK. Chicken. Call her. I've called old girl friends of mine. They're glad to hear from me.

NED. Well you, you stay so chummy with all your old girl friends. Who was it, Colleen? "Rick honey, we've got to stop seeing each other. I'm seeing someone else — the entire Yankee outfield." "Ok, Colleen, no problem." You didn't blink an eye.

RICK. Hey, they're my team.

NED. I need to hate just a little.

RICK. This is my philosophy on breaking up: There's no reason to burn bridges when you might want to get back on 'em

NED. Thank you for sharing that. I'm not going to call her.

RICK. Then you'll never see her again.

NED. (*A beat.*) Yes, I will.

RICK. You're going to call her?

NED. No.

RICK. She's going to call you?

NED. She'll never call me. We've got to meet on neutral territory.

RICK. Where's that?

NED. (*A beat.*) The "ten year."

RICK. The what?

NED. Our high school ten year reunion.

RICK. You're gonna sit around and wait for a high school reunion?

NED. I already did. It's next week.

RICK. I worry about you.

NED. You see, whenever Ellie and I said goodbye, we would pretend we wouldn't see each other again until the ten year. It was sort of a joke.

RICK. And you think for that very profound reason, she will attend.

NED. It is profound. Well ... It meant something to us. I know it did. If we're both so stubborn that neither one of us will make the first move, then the "ten year" might be neutral territory.

RICK. You think she's going to race up to you, look at the yearbook picture pinned to your chest, and say she's loved you all these years ... what a fool she's been?

NED. No. I don't think she'll do that. I do think it will give us a chance to talk. I know for certain that these last few years, she's missed me as much as I've missed her.

RICK. That's true. But that doesn't mean she'll go. I just don't picture Ellie as the sentimental type.

NED. Oh, she'll be there. I know it. (*A beat.*) What do you mean, "That's true."

RICK. Huh?

NED. You think she misses me too?

RICK. I do more than think it. I know it.

NED. How?

RICK. I saw Ellie a few months ago.

NED. You saw her!

RICK. In fact we had a drink together.

NED. You had a drink together! Why didn't you tell me this?

RICK. I thought you didn't want to be reminded of her. I didn't want to upset you.

NED. You're not. Tell me what happened. Where did you meet? When? Why?

RICK. Are you sure you want to hear?

NED. Just tell me.

RICK. We were both coming out of Astoria Studios.

(*ELLIE enters.*)

RICK. We both happened to be working on movies there.

NED. No. You were working on a *movie*. She was working on a *film*.

RICK. Ned, please don't interrupt. Well, we said our hellos ... She kissed me.

(*ELLIE kisses Rick.*)

NED. She kissed you?

RICK. Well, no. But if you can add a moon, I can add a kiss.

NED. Go on.

RICK. She looked like she wanted to talk more. So I said "Hey, you want to stop somewhere and have a drink." And she said ...
ELLIE. I think I'd like that.
RICK. So we did.

(*The LIGHTS come up on a small restaurant table. RICK and ELLIE sit.*)

NED. I can't believe you just ran into her. And that she'd actually be willing to stop and have a drink with you.
RICK. Ned, shhh ...
ELLIE. So, Rick, you look great.
RICK. Thanks. You look a little tired. Been working too hard?
ELLIE. I guess. Hey, chin, chin.

(*THEY toast.*)

NED. What was she drinking? Water, I bet.
RICK. Some kind of bubbly water.
NED. She drinks that, so that when you've had a few and begin to loosen up, she still has the upper hand.
RICK. Ned, please.
NED. God forbid she should loosen up.
RICK. Ned, shut up. You want to listen to this?
NED. To what?
ELLIE. Thanks for helping me get through the suicide hour.

RICK. The what?

ELLIE. They call this the suicide hour. More people kill themselves in the late afternoon than any other time of the day.

RICK. I guess that's why they invented happy hour.

ELLIE. When you think about it, there really isn't too much to do between five and seven ...

RICK. Except watch the news.

ELLIE. And kill yourself.

RICK. And drink cheap beer. (*To Ned.*) What do you make of all this?

NED. I'm not too sure. Sympathy, maybe.

RICK. You don't think she'd try to kill herself, do you?

NED. Ellie? Are you kidding? After a nuclear war, she'll be sweeping up. She's probably just rehearsing a scene from her new film.

ELLIE. So ... How's Ned doing?

NED. Well, I thought she'd never ask.

RICK. He's fine. (*A beat.*) So what's the movie you're working on?

NED. Is that all your going to say about me? You could at least talk about me for a minute.

RICK. Ned, would you let me play my scene?

ELLIE. It's a thriller. It's going to be good. I play a neurotic housewife.

NED. Who probably kills herself before dinner.

ELLIE. He's not married yet, is he?

RICK. Who? Ned? Nooo. Not yet.

NED. She's anxious for me to get married. Then I'll be "safe."

ELLIE. Is he seeing anyone?

RICK. Oh, I can't keep up with him. Let's see, there was Alice. She was ... French. Very exotic girl. The one before her must have been a model. She never ate anything. Right now he's seeing a woman named Nora. Very pretty. Very sophisticated. Very sweet.

NED. Thank you.

RICK. (*To Ned.*) You owe me one.

ELLIE. And what does Nora do? Another model?

RICK. No. She's a therapist. Makes top dollar, believe me.

ELLIE. Sounds like she'd be good for Ned.

NED. What's that supposed to mean?

RICK. What do you mean?

ELLIE. He was always interested in a girl he could settle down with. Get married. Maybe I should go have a talk with her.

NED. Huh?

ELLIE. There are times when I think that I need a therapist.

NED. Oh, please.

ELLIE. I don't know, Rick ... This is a tough business we've gotten into. Everyone wants a piece of you just because you can do the right tricks. You try to be everything to everybody. But you can't. Oh, you try to, but it gets harder and harder. Somewhere along the way, you stop, sit yourself down, and ask yourself, "Did I do the right thing? Am I doing the right thing now?" I don't know, Rick. I'd like so much to talk, but I haven't anybody.

(*Silence. After a moment, NED stands and applauds.*)

NED. Bravo! Bravo! I bet her parents never tied the knot. Tell me, was she munching a cucumber while she related this sob story? Perhaps cleaning a rifle. She wouldn't dare leave the house without her rifle. This was a performance, Rick. She's fooling you. This is her plea for human contact speech. She couldn't be vulnerable with anyone if she tried.

RICK. (*To Ned.*) Ned, I'm not stupid. She's not doing anything to me.

NED. (*Crosses to Ellie and looks in her eyes.*) Did she cry for you? She's good at that. She can cry on cue. Fake real tears.

RICK. She was not crying. She was just talking.

NED. She's fooling you into feeling sorry for her. She wants you to see her point of view.

RICK. All she's done so far, is show me how much she misses you. If she didn't miss you, do you think she would be sitting here chatting with me at all? She never liked me. I'm nothing more than a pipeline to you.

NED. An indirect pipeline. She wouldn't dare approach me directly.

RICK. And you won't approach her. Now do you want to hear this story, or not? Please, just let me tell you what she said to me.

(*NED sits back down.*)

RICK. Let's see, we had another drink. I asked her about her love life. She said ...

ELLIE. His name is Geoff.

RICK. Serious?

ELLIE. I guess.

RICK. Marriage?

ELLIE. Maybe. He's an exotic foreigner, too.

NED. He's probably going to be deported.

ELLIE. His green card expires soon. I may have to marry him to keep him in the country.

NED. True love. Leave it to Ellie to fall for an illegal alien. Don't have to worry about too much commitment there. Do we? (*Waving goodbye.*) "Bon voyage. Sorry it didn't work out." Nothing like subletting a relationship. We would want anyone to ask anything of us. We wouldn't want to have to open up and give anything to anyone. (*Losing it.*) Have I told you about some of the other guys she's seen? Ellie prefers a man with outside interests like ... men devoted to their wives ... or men devoted to God ... (*He crosses himself.*) Or men devoted to other men. If you told me you had six months to live – would I have a girl for you.

RICK. Ned! Stop. Why are you so bitter, so angry ...

NED. (*A beat.*) I'm angry because she still loves me, and she knows it. (*Shouting at Ellie.*) I am so angry with you. Damn you!

RICK. With me? Why are you angry with me?

NED. (*Calming down.*) I'm not. I'm sorry. Could you please leave me alone?

RICK. You ok?

NED. I'm fine. I just want to be left alone.

(*RICK exits. NED turns back to Ellie.*)

ELLIE. You know Ned, I really don't know what you're talking about. We have a good relationship. We get along. We have fun.

NED. I can't explain it. I see it. I know it's there.

ELLIE. That doesn't mean that I see it too.

NED. You do. I know you do. If you just let me in. Stop being so in check of your feelings. What are you afraid of?

ELLIE. I'm not afraid of anything. You know, I just hate it when you get like this. I see nothing wrong with things just the way they are.

(*Silence.*)

NED. Then I can't do this anymore. I can't be with you and pretend things are fine. I can't play with you whenever you feel like you need someone, and then go my merry way when you don't. I don't want to *not* see you anymore, but it's hurting me too much to hang around. I don't want to be anyone's companion.

ELLIE. (*A beat.*) All right then, go.

NED. You don't have anything to say?

ELLIE. What do I say? You're giving me this ultimatum.

NED. You don't understand, do you?

ELLIE. I do. You feel that you don't want to see me anymore, that's your decision. You do what you have to do. I'll do what I have to do.

NED. Don't do this.

ELLIE. What?

NED. You know what I mean.

ELLIE. No, I don't know.

(*THEY stare at each other a moment.*)

NED. Well ... I guess there's nothing more to say. (*A beat.*) See you at the "ten year." (*NED walks away from her.*)

ELLIE. Ned ... You can call me ... if you need to talk.

NED. (*Without turning around.*) I won't be doing that.

(*NED walks out. The LIGHTS on ELLIE fade out. NED wanders around in the dark, the LIGHTS eventually come up on the loft.*

NORA is seated on the couch. NED is still pacing. After some time ...)

NED. Well Doc, am I a looney tune?

NORA. *(Smiling.)* We try not to use the expression "looney tune." Try to think of yourself as still working things out.

NED. I won't sound as colorful, but I'll try it.

NORA. I'm glad you told me, Ned. Things make a little more sense now. I was beginning to think I was developing into a looney tune myself.

NED. No ... just me.

NORA. Besides, after hearing all about you and Eleanor, our parting of the ways seems rather calm.

NED. It's too bad we couldn't make a go of it.

NORA. I hope you're referring to us.

(HE smiles.)

NORA. I'd like to think you are. We both sort of knew it was the right thing to do. I'll be a wreck tomorrow ... but tonight, it feels right.

NED. If you want to call me up at any time, like to call me jerk names, feel free.

NORA. It's nice that you can still find humor...

NED. While I'm still working things out?

NORA. Yes. And I would love to take you up on that offer, but you're going out-of-town, remember?

NED. Do you think she'll be at this reunion?

NORA. It's not important what I think. If you believe she'll be there, then you need to go. (*SHE stands and kisses Ned on the cheek.*) And I do hope you find her.

NED. I'll see her. I don't know that I'll find her.

NORA. I keep seeing you, Ned, as that lonely gazebo from your photograph. I don't want to see you hurt.

NED. That's only because you know there's a bulldozer in the shadows. I only see the gazebo.

NORA. It's a fabulous view.

NED. They can't take that away from me.

NORA. I hope they never do. You give me hope. Somewhere out there is a guy kissing a pillow with my face on it.

(*NORA smiles, and exits. We hear airport NOISES, announcements, etc. The LIGHTS come up on the airport. NED picks up his suitcase and crosses to his gate. The LIGHTS on the loft fade. NED sits and waits for his flight. HE starts to fiddle with his camera. While playing with the focus, ELLIE enters. NED sees her through the lens. SHE looks altogether different. SHE has a small overnight bag. SHE stops and stares at him.*)

ELLIE. Neddie! Ned Edwards?

NED. (*Realizing.*) El? Ellie? Is that really you?

(*THEY embrace. Finally ...*)

ELLIE. (*Whispering to him.*) I've missed you so much.
NED. (*Whispering, too.*) I've missed you too.
ELLIE. (*Laughing.*) Neddie ...
NED. El, I can't believe it's you.
ELLIE. Did you think I was a figment of your imagination?
NED. Yes, actually.
ELLIE. How've you been?
NED. Good. You?
ELLIE. Never better.
NED. Look at you.
ELLIE. Same old Ned. Camera around his neck. Still seeing the world ...
NED. Out of focus.
ELLIE. Always working.
NED. Look who's talking. (*A pause.*) Whoa.
ELLIE. My heart is absolutely racing.
NED. Mine too.

(*THEY stare. Smile. And then hug again.*)

ELLIE. You still smell the same way.
NED. Hey, thanks.

ELLIE. No. I mean a good smell. Your smell. I haven't smelled it since ... I can't remember. How's your family?

NED. Good. Real good. Yours?

ELLIE. Fine. Just fine. Your grandmother? She still as feisty as ever?

NED. Until the day she died.

ELLIE. I'm sorry.

NED. It's all right. Thanks. (*A beat.*) So how you doin'?

ELLIE. Real well. Things have been so hectic these last few months. I'm having contract problems. They want to extend the play. I have a film that starts shooting in six weeks. I'm still doing promos for the last one. I tell you, Ned, I can't keep up. If I had know it would be this much work, I would have had you try and talk me out of it. How about you? How're you doing?

NED. Still smiling.

(*THEY smile at one another.*)

ELLIE. You married yet?

NED. No. (*A pause.*) I thought about you the other day.

ELLIE. Really?

NED. I came across the old Gershwin album.

ELLIE. Oh, God, not that. That goes way back. How can you remember that?

NED. I remember a lot of things. Photographic memory, I guess.

(*SHE laughs.*)

NED. We knocked that couch over so often, the neighbors started to complain ...

ELLIE. Well, we were young and foolish.

NED. Perhaps. (*A beat.*) Come on, let's do it. The topper. We'll knock a row of seats over.

ELLIE. Ned, we're in an airport.

NED. You're right, they're probably glued down.

ELLIE. Neddie, you haven't changed at all. You're still such a clown.

NED. It will be good to see everyone again. Some of the gang I haven't seen since graduation.

ELLIE. Where were you last night? You missed John's party.

NED. I know. I had some editing to do. Couldn't get away till today ... You went to the party last night?

ELLIE. It was great. Everyone was there. Except you.

NED. Wait, you're getting *off* a plane. You've already been home. (*A beat.*) Then you're not going to the reunion tonight?

ELLIE. No. I thought I might see you last night. Isn't it strange running into you today?

NED. It certainly is. The reunion is in four hours. You couldn't stay another night?

ELLIE. Well, I had this flight booked.

NED. Well, you could have changed it?

ELLIE. Ned, do you really want to go to a high school reunion?

NED. Looks that way, doesn't it? I thought I'd go just to see who shows up.

(*Silence.*)

ELLIE. Isn't this just like us to run into each other in the airport. We must stop meeting like this.

NED. Right.

ELLIE. I hope your flight is better than mine was. The studio goofed up and I had to sit all the way in the back ... Don't you just hate that?

NED. Just hate it.

ELLIE. It wouldn't be so bad if people would leave you alone. But they don't. Anybody who recognizes you feels like they have to come up and say hello ...

NED. And make you autograph their boarding pass. You poor thing.

ELLIE. My name on a piece of paper? Neddie, come on. I'm an actress, not a celebrity.

NED. True. It won't be long before you have your own salad dressing.

ELLIE. I'm sorry. What?

NED. Nothing.

ELLIE. Listen, I've got to run. I've got someone meeting me downstairs.

NED. Was that your Kamikazie pilot in baggage claim?

ELLIE. (*Not getting it.*) Neddie, you're still so funny. It's great to see you again.

NED. Good seeing you.

ELLIE. Say, let's get together sometime.

NED. Sure.

ELLIE. Where can I reach you?

NED. Same place I've always been.

ELLIE. Good. We'll keep in touch. I gotta run. So long.

NED. So long.

(*ELLIE exits. NEDDIE watches her go. Finally...*)

NED. See you at the "twenty-fifth!"

(*NED sits back down and waits for the flight. After a moment, RICK enters.*)

RICK. I know you're a big boy. You've gotten on airplanes before. But I couldn't just drop you. I parked the car and came in. I just thought ... well, she might be on your flight.

NED. I wouldn't bet on it.

RICK. I mean you're both going to the same place. And this is probably the last flight you can take.

NED. She's not going to the reunion.

RICK. She's not? How do you know?

NED. She was just here. You just missed her.

RICK. She came to see you off?

NED. She's already been home. And would you believe that she wouldn't hang out a few extra hours to go to the reunion? I mean she made a conscious decision not to go. She's afraid that hundreds of former high school friends might attack her, and ask for her autograph ... forgetting, of course, that most of us already have that treasured signature, complete with dotted smiley face, in our yearbooks. I should have signed hers, "Manon to Marguerite — Humilité."

RICK. I'm sorry, Ned. I don't know Latin.

NED. Don't be sorry. I'm glad I saw her. If I'd gone to the reunion and not seen her, I would have made up an excuse for her. But for her to be right there, and not stay another few hours — the event itself meant nothing to her.

RICK. What did she say?

NED. It was tense there for a while but after we started talking ... nothing's changed. (*Blowing it off.*) Whew!

RICK. Hey, no problem. Give Nora a call. Tell her you're not going home ...

NED. I don't know if that's such a good idea.

RICK. You don't want to see her anymore?

NED. Well ... I'm not burning any bridges.

RICK. I know *I'm* not seeing her anymore.

NED. You're cured? You're able to take a shower alone now?

RICK. No. But Nora wants me to stop making slasher movies. She feels that if I work on more artistic films, I will have more self esteem ...

NED. And eventually be able to shower alone.

RICK. The only problem with achieving all that integrity in your work, is that when you come right down to it, I like blood and guts better. Besides, the girls are prettier in the butcher movies than they are in "Gandhi." So I guess I'm stuck in the tub ...

BOTH. Or showering with someone else.

(*THEY laugh.*)

RICK. All right. Here's what we do. If we hurry, we can catch the last half of the game on TV. It's a double-header. We grab a pizza, couple of six-packs. Tomorrow we grab the binocs and go to the beach. You'll forget all about the reunion. What do you say?

NED. Rick ... you're a good friend. You have limited interests, but you are a good friend.

RICK. They may be limited, but they're choice.

NED. If it's all the same to you, I think I'll still go to the reunion. It still means something to me. (*A beat.*) Hey, why don't you get out of here. I have this plane to wait for and you probably have a date.

(*RICK stands.*)

NED. Thanks.

RICK. Ned, if this is any help ... what convinced me to ignore my fear of showering alone ... If you think about what's troubling you ... on close inspection, it's probably just Jello with baked beans in it.
NED. (*Smiling.*) Get out of here.
RICK. I'm going. I'm going.

(*RICK exits. NED stands and heads towards his gate. ELLIE enters. SHE puts her hand in the air.*)

ELLIE. Edna St. Vincent Millay!
NED. (*Spins around.*) Did you change your mind?

(*ELLIE smiles and waves at Ned.*)

NED. Oh, it's you. What are you doing here?
ELLIE. Keeping you company.
NED. For some reason, after the cold wind blew through, I thought I would never see you again.
ELLIE. She's not right for you, Ned.
NED. I can't think why I've been so stuck on you all these years. I thought for sure you were the girl for me.
ELLIE. I am the girl for you. If I wasn't, why else would I be hanging around airports?
NED. Huh?

ELLIE. I'm not her, Ned. You just make me look like her. You know that. Ellie doesn't get the joke anymore.

NED. No. I was counting on it though. Didn't you think she would change?

ELLIE. I sort of think what *you* think.

(*THEY both laugh.*)

NED. How come you couldn't look like Nora?

ELLIE. I don't know. I tried. I just couldn't do it. Maybe it was that nightgown ...

NED. Could you do me a favor?

ELLIE. That's what I'm here for.

NED. The next time I conjure you, could you come back as a redhead? I've always fancied myself with a redhead. A tall redhead.

ELLIE. Who doesn't?

NED. Am I doing it again? Wanting too much? I just see how terrific it all can be.

ELLIE. You're in love with someone you haven't met yet.

NED. (*Picks up his suitcase.*) You coming with?

ELLIE. I think I'm going to hang back. Get cleaned up ... Get out of these old clothes.

NED. Put on a new face ...

ELLIE. Hey, I might just surprise you. I could be that redhead sitting next to you on the plane.

NED. I just hope you won't be tattooed, or speak in tongues ...

ELLIE. Ned ... Let's just hope I'm female and build up from there. Ok?

NED. Ok.

ELLIE. Hey, Ned, catch you at that "ten year."

(SHE smiles and turns to exit. NED heads off towards his plane. HE stops and shouts off towards Ellie.)

NED. Oh, please ... Please don't be Rosamund Threlkeld. Please.

ELLIE. (*Stops.*) She always liked you.

NED. Please not Rosie Threlkeld ...

ELLIE. Ned, it's been ten years ... (*A beat.*) Wait till you see her!

(SHE leaves. After a second ... NED smiles, grabs his bag and walks slowly upstage into the darkness. After he has disappeared, a large MOON appears. The LIGHTS fade.)

THE END

COSTUME PLOT

NED – He's a sharp dresser, but not eclectic, and not preppie. Since he has little time to change his clothes, he needs pants that will go with a sweater in the opening, a Yankee jacket at the ball park, jacket and tie for the restaurant, etc.

In Act II he wears a smoking jacket and dark sweatpants. He changes into shirt and pants for the rest of the play. At the airport, he adds a jacket.

ELLIE – Since Ellie dresses as Ned remembers her, she too, dresses smartly. At the opening of Act I, she's wearing slacks and a sweater. She changes into a dress for the restaurant scene. At the end of Act I, when she is not a memory, Ned's imagination might dress her in something that Carole Lombard or Claudette Colbert would wear to lounge around the penthouse.

At the opening of Act II, she wears a floor-length robe. Again, something from the thirties, yet a robe that Ellie could truly own. For *The Cherry Orchard* scene, she wears full turn-of-the-century costume and for the island, "photograph," she wears a swim suit. For Rick's restaurant scene, she wears a skirt and blouse. For the airport scene, she wears a hat and a reversible raincoat. When she returns for the last scene, she flips the raincoat to the other side and carries the hat.

NORA – She probably devotes a lot of time to planning her wardrobe. Her shoes, scarves, etc. all match. She wears a dress on her date with Ned. In Act II, she wears a nightgown. She changes into a suit for the therapy session and back into a dress for her last scene.

RICK – In Act I, he wears black jeans, a Hawaiian shirt and gym shoes. In Act II, a different Hawaiian shirt.

ANDREA – She's the type who would dress in leather, if it didn't make her sneeze.

ALICE – Anything frilly.

PROPERTY LIST

Playscript (ELLIE)
Bag of vegetables (NED)
Gourd (NED)
Cucumbers (NED and ELLIE)
Camera (NED)
Pillows
Black fedora hat (NED)
Sunglasses (NED)
Glass of water (NED)
Slides
Light box
Loupe
Binoculars (RICK)
Hot dogs (NED)
Burgundy wine glasses
Bordeaux bottle
Silverware for 2
Napkins (2)
Menus (3)
Popcorn (RICK)
Glasses of port (2)
Port decanter
Ned's portfolio
Photographs of Ellie
Tray of slides
Candles
Bedspread
VCR remote control (RICK)
Rifle (ELLIE)

Rolling cart with darkroom supplies, trays, solutions, etc.
Beer bottles (NED and RICK)
Palm tree cut out
Glass of water (ELLIE)
Suitcase (NED)
Overnight bag (ELLIE)

Other Publications for Your Interest

ALONE AT THE BEACH
(LITTLE THEATRE—COMEDY)
By RICHARD DRESSER

4 men, 3 women—Combination Interior/Exterior

"So you thought the kind of comedy that sends audiences home happy had disappeared from the American theatre scene? *"Wrong!"* enthused the Louisville Courier-Journal over this literate, witty comedy, which had the audience at Actors Theatre of Louisville's famed Humana Festival whooping with laughter. George, a mild-mannered man in his mid-30's, has inherited a beach house in the Hamptons on Long Island. In order to afford to keep it, he has let out rooms to boarders, Manhattan-ites desparate to get out of the city on weekends. Blindly, and blithely, George has not actually *met* any of these denizens of the yuppie sector of the urban jungle. If everyone were Great Fun and Easy To Get Along With, everyone would have a great time—but the audience, of course, wouldn't. Who wants to watch a bunch of friendly, well-adjusted people have Fun In The Sun? Thankfully, Dresser gives us a motley crew of urban neurotics, male and female, who begin to drive George, and everyone else, crazy the moment they arrive. Somehow, though, everyone survives the experience, egos intact; and, in fact, some of the most unlikely romances develop, before everyone has to face reality: Labor Day and, subsequently, the trek back to New York City for good—until next summer? "Has a unique sparkle." New Albany Tribune. "A winner...a riotously funny sex farce."—Detroit News. "A charming romp that should turn up in regional and community theatres all over the place."—Houston Post. "Has the pacing of a Neil Simon script but with some of the dry, more cerebral wit of Jules Feiffer."—Evansville Courier.

(#3118)

EMILY
(ADVANCED GROUPS—SERIOUS COMEDY)
By STEPHEN METCALFE

8 men, 4 women, to play a variety of roles.
Bare stage, w/drops, wings, projections & wagons; or, may be unit set.

This brilliant, cynical, contemporary new comedy by the author of *Strange Snow, Vikings, Sorrows and Sons* and *The Incredibly Famous Willy Rivers* dares to take what amounts to a politically "incorrect" stance about the successful "New Woman." Emily is a successful New York City stockbroker who mixes it up with the boys and always comes out on top. In fact, she was described by one misguided critic as coming off like a "man in drag"; because, as we all know, women are caring, loving, nurturing creatures—and what a wonderful world it would be if *they* were in positions of political and/or business power, instead of those insensitive jerks, the *men*. Emily is just as cynical and ruthless as any man in her position; until, that is, she meets a caring, sensitive, aspiring actor (in other words, a nice guy with no money) who doesn't fall for her manipulative ruses; but, rather, for the real Emily he sees inside the ruthless yuppie—who may, or may not, exist. "Glorious...a sparkling comedy with bite to it. The title character is a gold mine of a role for an actress."— San Diego Tribune. "A real winner...a bravura balancing act right on the edge of sentimentality, finally and triumphantly crystalline in its emotional honesty...A triumph." —San Diego Union.

(#7076)

Other Publications for Your Interest

THE VOICE OF THE PRAIRIE
(LITTLE THEATRE—COMIC/DRAMA)
By JOHN OLIVE

2 men, 1 women—to play a variety of roles
May be done with up to 10 actors—Unit Setting

When this play begins, we are listening to an old hobo (named "Poppy" by his avid companion young Davey Quinn) tell a tall tale. It is the early 1890's, and itinerant story tellers such as Poppy really were the voices of the prairie. Many years later, when Davey is grown up, he is "discovered" by radio entrepreneur Leon Schwab, telling his tales of Poppy and of Frankie the Blind Girl, whom he rescued from a cruel father and with whom he went on a cross-country adventure. Schwab thinks Quinn's stories would attract an audience for radio, the "wave of the future". Sure enough, David Quinn becomes famous as the Voice of the Prairie, as the cleverly-constructed play cross-cuts between scenes of Leon and David and scenes of young Davey and Frankie the Blind Girl, on the lam, in search of adventure. These scenes culminate in the unfortunate separation of Davey and Frankie, as Frankie is recognized, captured and sent back home. David Quinn, the grown-up Voice of the Prairie, has not seen or heard from her since; until, that is, Leon locates her in hopes of using his discovery of the actual, famous Frankie the Blind Girl for its sentimental value, to keep the new F.C.C. off his back. Will David forgive Frankie for leaving him so many years ago? Will Frankie agree to help Leon avoid jail for broadcasting without a license? "Endearing."—N.Y. Times. "That rare thing: a small, skillful play with a deft heart."—Los Angeles Times. "Beguiling entertainment and as American as corn."—Hartford Advocate. "First-rate entertainment. I can't remember when I last so enjoyed a play."—Torrington Register Citizen. Slightly Restricted.

(#24047)

CARELESS LOVE
(LITTLE THEATRE—DRAMA)
By JOHN OLIVE

1 male, 1 woman—Unit set

What a terrific little play for an actress and actor to sink their teeth into! And, it's about something that matters: commitment, and responsibility, in love. When we first meet Jack, he is an aspiring actor, serious about his career but not very serious about his girlfriend, Martha, a waitress who is an aspiring dancer, who is a lot more serious about Jack. The couple drifts along on a cloud of good times — until Martha gets pregnant, at which time a *Choice* must be made. As the debate over their options progresses, Jack's acting career starts to take off; and, he starts to think more seriously about his life and his responsibilities. Unfortunately, at the same time Martha has been driven into self-absorption by Jack's carelessness, and has made a decision which is right for her, she thinks: she has decided to give the child up for adoption. So — at just about the time Jack is ready to make an emotional committment to Martha and to their child, it is too late: Martha has had the baby and put it up for adoption. This was, after all, *her* decision to make. Right? In the end, Martha is a self-sufficient contemporary woman, who makes her own choices. It is Jack who will hurt forever, from the pain of eternal separation from his child. "Bittersweet." — Variety. "In the delicacy of its writing, in the truth of its details...it is a most lovely, most satisfying evening in the theatre."—Chicago Tribune. "A lovely little play...works a winsome magic."—Philadelphia Daily News.

(#5237)